GHOSTL

The remarkable revival of interest in ghost stories at the present time is curious, for ghost stories traditionally belong to that great age of story telling: the 19th century. And yet, despite the distractions of the television screen, ghost stories are much in demand, particularly among the young. Here you will find examples of ghost stories ranging from R. L. Stevenson and J. S. LeFanu in the 19th century to the most contemporary of contemporary writers—Alan Garner and Joan Aiken.

Some of the stories are truly spine-chillers; some of the ghosts are gentle, some are not; but the collection should provide plenty of ghostly 'pleasure'.

'A splendid collection of supernatural adventures.'
New Statesman

'The stories in this collection have been chosen with discrimination and illustrated with a sure intuition.'
Growing Point

Ghostly Experiences and *Ghostly Encounters*, also an Armada Lion, were published as a single volume in hardback under the title *The Restless Ghost*.

Also published as
an Armada Lion by Susan Dickinson

GHOSTLY ENCOUNTERS

GHOSTLY EXPERIENCES

Chosen by

SUSAN DICKINSON

Illustrated by

Antony Maitland

COLLINS

ARMADA LIONS

First published 1970 as part of the collection, *The Restless Ghost*
by William Collins Sons & Co Ltd
14 St James's Place, London, SW1
First published in Armada Lions 1972
Second Impression April 1973

Printed in Great Britain
by William Collins Sons & Co Ltd, Glasgow

CONTENTS

ACKNOWLEDGMENTS

The Editor and Publishers are grateful to the following for permission to reprint copyright material in this anthology:

The author for *Feel Free* © 1968 by Alan Garner;

A. M. Heath and Co. Ltd. for *Minuke* by Nigel Kneale © 1949 by Nigel Kneale;

The Executors of William Croft Dickinson for *The Witch's Bone* from *Dark Encounters* published by the Harvill Press © 1963 by William Croft Dickinson;

Curtis Brown Ltd. for *Lucky's Grove* by H. R. Wakefield from *The Clock Strikes Twelve*;

Scott Meredith Ltd. for *The Moon Bog* by H. P. Lovecraft;

A. M. Heath and Co. Ltd. for *The Apple of Trouble* by Joan Aiken © 1968 by Joan Aiken.

Feel Free

ALAN GARNER

The line of sight from Tosh's den to Brian went under the Giant Panda's belly, between the gilded coffin of Bak-en-Mut and the town stocks, through the Taj Mahal and over Lady Henrietta Maria's dyed bodice. The first morning when Brian had started his drawing the Taj Mahal had blocked Tosh's view, but when Brian came back from his dinner three doors had opened to give a clear run through, and whenever he looked Tosh's eye was on him.

Tosh kept to his den, where he brewed tea and

filled in his coupon, unless he was on patrol. He patrolled every hour, on the hour, up one side, across the back and down the other side, which meant that he came upon Brian from behind. He said nothing the first day, but stood at ease, lifting his heels and lowering them; click; click; click; and he sucked his teeth. Then he patrolled back to his den. There were no visitors to the museum all day, all week.

'What are you on?' said Tosh half-way through the second afternoon.

'Eh up,' said Brian. 'It talks.'

'None of your lip,' said Tosh. His medal ribbons bristled.

But on the third day Tosh patrolled with a mug of hot brown water thickened with condensed milk. 'Cuppertea,' he said.

Brian put down his drawing board. 'Thanks, Tosh.'

'Yer welcome.'

'How's trade?' said Brian.

'Average,' said Tosh. 'For the season.'

'Been pretty quiet here, hasn't it?' said Brian. 'Since they built the Holiday Camp, I mean. The old park just can't compete, can it?'

'We have our regulars,' said Tosh. 'And our aberlutions is still second to none.'

'It's Open Day up the Camp,' said Brian. 'Anyone can go, free.'

'It's all kidology,' said Tosh. 'There's nowt free in this world, lad.'

'There is today,' said Brian. 'I'm going, anyroad.'

'What are you on here?' said Tosh.

'It's my Project for school,' said Brian. 'Last term it was Compost: this term it's Pottery.'

The next time round Tosh said, 'What you got to do with this malarky?'

'I'm trying to draw that Ancient Greek dish from all sides and see if I can copy it.'

'What for?'

'Greek pottery's supposed to be the best, so I thought I'd start at the top.'

'Fancy it, do you?'

'Yes,' said Brian. 'It's funny, is that. I seem to be quite knacky with it, though I've only just started. I may go and do evening classes.'

'I'm partial to a bit of art, meself,' said Tosh. 'Sign-writing: but painting's favourite. Not yon modern stuff, though: more traditional—dogs and flowers and that. It makes you realise how much work they put in, them fellers. Same as him there.' Tosh pointed to the Egyptian coffin. 'Yon Back-in-a-Minute. The gold leaf and stuff, all them little pictures—that wasn't done on piece work. Eh? Not on piece work.'

'Not this dish, neither,' said Brian. 'That's why I'm having such a sweat over the drawing. Every line's perfect.'

'Ah,' said Tosh. 'They had time in them days. They had all the time there is. All the time in the world.'

The dish stood alone in its case, a typed label on the glass: 'Attic Krater, 5th Century BC, Artist Unknown. The scene depicts Charon, ferryman of the dead, conveying a soul across the river Acheron in the Underworld.'

At first Brian had thought the design was too wooden and formal. The old boatman Charon crouched with bent knees, and the dead man was as blank as any traveller. The waves curled in solid, regular spirals and the rest of the design was geometry—squares, crosses, leaf patterns without life. But as he worked Brian found a balance and a rhythm in the dish. Nothing was there without a reason, and its place in the design was so accurately fixed that to move it was like playing a wrong note. And all this Brian had found in two days from a red and black dish in a glass case.

'Have you done, then?' said Tosh an hour later.

Brian sat with his hands in his pockets, glaring at the dish.

'No. Eh, Tosh: let's have the case open. I want to cop hold of that dish.'

'Not likely,' said Tosh. 'It's more than my job's worth. Can't you see all you want from here?'

'Seeing's not enough. That's why these drawings don't work. They're on the flat, and the dish is curved. Pattern and shape are all part of it—you can't have one without the other. My drawing's like sucking sweets with the wrapper on.'

'What if you bust it, though?' said Tosh.

'It'd mend. It's been bust before. Come on, Tosh, be a pal.'

Tosh went to his den and came back with a key. 'I know nowt about this,' he said.

Brian moved his fingers along the surfaces of the dish. 'That's it,' he kept saying. 'That's it. Yes. That's it. Eh, Tosh, the man as made this was a blooming marvel. It's perfect. It's like I don't know what, it's like—it's—heck, it's like flying.'

'Ay, well, one thing's for sure,' said Tosh. 'The feller as made yon: his head doesn't ache. How old is it?'

'A good two thousand year,' said Brian. 'Two thousand year. He sat and worked this out, these curves and lines and colours and patterns, and then he made it. Two thousand year. Heck. And it's come all that way. To me. So as I know what he was thinking. Two thousand . . .'

'Ay, his head doesn't ache any more, right enough,' said Tosh.

Brian turned the cup over to examine the base.

'It'd do for a cake stand, would that,' said Tosh. 'For Sundays.'

'Tosh, look!' Brian nearly dropped the dish. On the

base was a clear thumb print fired hard as the rest of the clay.

'There he is,' whispered Brian.

The change from the case to the outside air had put a mist on the surface of the dish, and Brian set his own fingers against the other hand.

'Two thousand year, Tosh. That's nothing. Who was he?'

'No, he'll not have a headache.'

Brian stared at his own print and the fossilled clay. 'Tosh,' he said, 'they're the same. That thumb print and mine. What do you make of it?'

'They're not,' said Tosh. 'No two people ever has the same tabs.'

'These are.'

'They can't be,' said Tosh. 'I went on courses down London when I was a constable.'

'These are the same.'

'You might think so, but you'd be wrong. It's been proved as how every man, woman and child is born with different finger prints from anyone else.'

'How's it been proved?' said Brian.

'Because the same prints have never turned up twice. Why, men have been hanged on the strength of that, and where would be the sense if it wasn't true?'

'Look for yourself,' said Brian.

Tosh put on his glasses. For a while he said nothing, then, 'Ah. Very good. Very close, I'll allow, but see at yon line across the other feller's thumb. That's a scar. You haven't got one.'

'But a scar's something that happens,' said Brian. 'It's nothing to do with what you're born like. If he hadn't gashed his thumb, they'd be the same.'

'But they're not, are they?' said Tosh. 'And it was a long time ago, so what's the odds?'

Brian finished his drawings early. He was taking

Sandra to the Open Day at the Camp, and he wanted to have a shave. They met at the bus stop.

'There's that Beryl Fletcher,' said Sandra.

'What about her?' said Brian.

'She only left school last week, and she's cracking on she's dead sophisticated.'

'Give over,' said Brian. 'You're jealous.'

Two buses came and went.

'Do you like me dress?' said Sandra.

'Yes.'

'Just "yes"?'

'It's all right,' said Brian. 'Smashing.'

'You never noticed,' said Sandra.

'I did. It's nice—better than Beryl Fletcher's.'

Sandra laughed. 'You'd never notice, you great cloth-head. What's up? You've not had two words to say for yourself.'

'Sorry,' said Brian. 'I was thinking about that dish I've been working on all week at the museum.'

'What's her name?'

'I don't know her name, but she's very mature.'

'How old is she?' said Sandra.

'Two-and-a-bit-thousand year.'

A bus came and they got on.

'You know Tosh, the head Parky, him as looks after the museum?' said Brian.

'Yes. He's our kid's wife's uncle.'

'Was he ever a bobby?'

'He used to be a sergeant,' said Sandra.

Three stops later Sandra said, 'You're quiet.'

'Am I? Sorry.'

'What's to do, love? What's wrong?'

'Have you ever hidden something to chance it being found again years and years later—perhaps long after you're dead?'

'No,' said Sandra.

'I have,' said Brian. 'I was a great one for filling screw-top bottles with junk and then burying them. I put notes inside, and pieces out of the newspaper. You're talking to somebody you'll never meet, never know: but if they find the bottle they'll know you. There's bits of you in the bottle, waiting all this time, see, in the dark, and as soon as the bottle's opened—time's nothing—and—and—'

'Eh up,' said Sandra, 'people are looking. You do get some ideas, Brian Walton!'

'It's that dish at the museum,' said Brian. 'I thought it was a crummy old pot, but when I started to sort it out I found what was inside it.'

'What? A message?' said Sandra.

'No. Better than that. This fellow as made it over two thousand years ago—he knew nothing about me, but he worked out how to fit the picture and the shape together. When you look at it you don't see how clever he was, but when you touch it, and try to copy it, you're suddenly with him,—same as if you're watching over his shoulder and he's talking to you, showing you. So when I do a pot next, he'll be helping. It'll be his pot. And he's been dead two thousand year! What about that, eh?'

'Fancy,' said Sandra.

The bus had arrived at the camp. Sandra was about to step down from the platform when she tipped forward at the waist. Her eyes widened and she clutched at the rail.

'What's the matter?' said Brian.

'It's me shoe!' she hissed. 'It's fast!' The stiletto heel had jammed between the ridges of the platform, and Sandra had to take her shoe off to get it free. 'Oh, it's scratched!' she said. 'First time out, and all.'

'Come on,' said Brian. 'If you will be sophisticated . . .'

'Hello! Hello! Hello!' said the loudspeaker. 'This is Open Day, friends, and it's free, free, free! Walk in! Have fun!'

'Where do you want to start?' said Brian.

'I don't know,' said Sandra. 'Let's see what there is.'

'Hello! Hello! Hello! This is Your Day and Your Camp. The Camp with a Difference, friends and neighbours, Where Only You Matter. This is the Camp with Only One Rule—Feel Free! Feel free, friends!'

Brian and Sandra danced to two of the five resident tape recordings, drove a motor boat on the Marine Lake, spun their own candy floss . . .

'Hello! Hello! Hello! Feel free, friends! This is the Lay-Say-Fair Holiday Camp, a totally new concept in Family Camping, adding a new dimension to leisure, where folk come to stay, play, make hay, or relax in the laze-away-days that you find only at the Lay-Say-Fair Holiday Camp. Yes! And it's all free, friends. Thanks to the All-in L.S.F. Tariff, which you pay when you reserve your chalet. There are no hidden extras: this once-and-for-all payment is your passport to delight. Yes! Remember! L.S.F. saves L.S.D.! Now!'

'Me feet are killing me,' said Sandra.

They sat on a bench in the Willow Pattern Garden. Brian stroked the head of a Chinese bronze dragon, from which the Camp's music tinkled. The sun was low, the day at its best after the heat.

'Isn't it dreamy?' said Sandra. 'Better than the old park. These banks and banks of flowers and rock gardens: and the bees buzzing.'

'It's hard luck on the bees,' said Brian. 'They'll be dead by morning.'

'You're proper cheerful today, you are,' said Sandra. 'Why will they be dead?'

'Selective weedkiller,' said Brian. 'You couldn't keep the soil as clean as that, else. They spray it on, and nobody bothers to tell the bees.'

'How do you know?'

'I read quite a lot about it last term,' said Brian. 'When I was doing Compost. There's a lot in soil; you may not think it, but there is.'

'We're off,' said Sandra.

'No. Look,' said Brian, and leant backwards to gather a handful of earth from a rockery flower bed. 'Soil isn't muck, it's . . . well, I'll be . . . Sandra? This here soil's plastic!'

Smooth, clean granules rolled between his fingers.

'The whole blooming lot's plastic—grass, flowers, and all!'

'Now that's what I call sensible. It helps to keep the cost down,' said Sandra. 'And it doesn't kill bees.'

'Ay,' said Brian. 'Bees. Surely they're not that daft.'

He climbed up the rockery, and he soon found the bees. They were each mounted on a quivering hair spring, the buzzer plugged in to a time switch.

'Hello! Hello! Hello!' said the bronze dragon. 'Lay-Say-Fair, The Camp with a Difference. Have you visited the Pleasureteria yet, friends? The L.S.F. Pleasureteria is the only Do-if-Yourself Fun-Drome in existence: all the fun of the fair for free! Free! Now!'

'We'll have a stab at that, shall we?' said Brian.

They rode on the Big Wheel, the Dodgems, the Roller Coaster, the Dive Bomber, the Octopus. The equipment was automatically controlled. Lights winked, recorded voices gave instructions, bells rang.

In the Pally-Palais Sandra battled with sudden air jets from the floor, and clung to Brian on the Cake Walk. It was late dusk when they came out of the Palais. They laughed a lot.

'Well, something's made you buck up at last,' said Sandra. 'I thought I was landed with pottery and compost for the night.'

'What shall we go on now?' said Brian.

'There's the Tunnel of Love, if you're feeling romantic,' said Sandra.

'You never know till you try, do you?' said Brian.

They walked on to the stage by the water channel. There was a gate across the channel with a notice saying: 'Passengers wait here. Pull illuminated handle for boat. Do not board boat until boat has stopped. Do not stand up in boat. Passengers must be seated when bell rings. No smoking.'

' "Feel free, friends",' said Brian.

Beyond the gate was a grotto of plaster stalactites and stalagmites, and the channel rushed among them to a black tunnel.

'Queer green light there, isn't it?' said Sandra. 'Ever so eerie.'

'Special paint,' said Brian. 'It shows up luminous in ultra-violet light. Remember that Bottom of the Sea Spectacular in "Goldilocks on Ice" at the Opera House last year? Same thing in this grotto.'

Brian pulled the lever and a boat came out of the darkness upstream. Its prow was shaped to fit in a recess in the gate, which kept it firm.

'Passengers board now,' said a recorded voice. 'Take your seats immediately. Passengers board now. Take your seats immediately. Do not stand.'

Brian climbed into the boat and turned to help Sandra. She put one foot on the seat, then twisted awkwardly.

'Hurry up,' said Brian.

'It's me heel again. It's caught in something. On the stage.'

They began to laugh. Brian tried to lift Sandra into the boat but had nothing to brace himself against.

'Kick your shoe off.'

'I can't.'

They pushed and pushed. A bell rang. 'All passengers sit. Stand clear. Do not try to board. Stand clear.'

The bell rang again, and the gate flew open.

Sandra was still laughing, but Brian felt the water take the boat, and he knew he could not hold it. Already he was being dragged off balance.

'Get back,' he said. 'You'll fall in. Get back.'

'I can't, I'm stuck.'

'I'm going to shove you,' said Brian. 'Shove you. Ready? On three. One. Two. Three. . . .!'

He pushed Sandra as hard as he could, and she fell back on to the stage. He lurched in the boat and grabbed at the stern to save himself. For a moment the boat hung level with Sandra, who was three feet away, but dry, as she scrambled up, still laughing.

'Enjoy yourself!' she shouted. The boat bobbed away on the race, and Brian stood watching. Now he was in the grotto, and Sandra was distant in another light.

'Sit down, Brian! Coo-ee! Have a nice trip, love, and if you can't be good be careful! Shall I see you next time round? Coo-ee!'

She was swinging away from him, a tiny figure lost among stalactites. He stood, looking, looking, and slowly lifted his hand off the nail that had worked loose at the edge of the stern. He had not felt its sharpness, but now the gash throbbed across the ball of his thumb. The boat danced towards the tunnel.

Minuke

NIGEL KNEALE

The estate agent kept an uncomfortable silence until we had reached his car. 'Frankly, I wish you hadn't got wind of that,' he said. 'Don't know how you did: I thought I had the whole thing carefully disposed of. Oh, please get in.'

He pulled his door shut and frowned. 'It puts me in a rather awkward spot. I suppose I'd better tell you all I know about that case, or you'd be suspecting me of heaven-knows-what kinds of chicanery in your own.'

As we set off to see the property I was interested in, he shifted the cigarette to the side of his mouth.

'It's quite a distance, so I can tell you on the way there,' he said. 'We'll pass the very spot, as a matter of fact, and you can see it for yourself. Such as there is to see.'

*

It was away back before the war (said the estate agent). At the height of the building boom. You remember how it was: ribbon development in full blast everywhere; speculative builders sticking things up almost overnight. Though at least you could get a house when you wanted it in those days.

I've always been careful in what I handle—I want you to understand that. Then one day I was handed a packet of coast-road bungalows, for letting. Put up by one of these gone tomorrow firms, and bought by a local man. I can't say I exactly jumped for joy, but for once the things looked all right, and—business is inclined to be business.

The desirable residence you heard about stood at the

end of the row. Actually, it seemed to have the best site. On a sort of natural platform, as it were, raised above road level and looking straight out over the sea. Like all the rest, it had a simple two-bedroom, lounge, living-room, kitchen, bathroom layout. Red-tiled roof, roughcast walls. Ornamental portico, garden strip all round. Sufficiently far from town, but with all conveniences.

It was taken by a man named Pritchard. Cinema projectionist, I think he was. Wife, a boy of ten or so, and a rather younger daughter. Oh—and dog, one of those black, lop-eared animals. They christened the place 'Minuke', M-I-N-U-K-E. My Nook. Yes, that's what I said too. And not even the miserable excuse of its being phonetically correct. Still, hardly worse than most.

Well, at the start everything seemed quite jolly. The Pritchards settled in and busied themselves with rearing a privet hedge and shoving flowers in. They'd paid the first quarter in advance, and as far as I was concerned, were out of the picture for a bit.

Then, about a fortnight after they'd moved in, I had a telephone call from Mrs P to say there was something odd about the kitchen tap. Apparently the thing had happened twice. The first time was when her sister was visiting them, and tried to fill the kettle: no water would come through for a long time, then suddenly squirted violently and almost soaked the woman. I gather the Pritchards hadn't really believed this—thought she was trying to find fault with their little nest—it had never happened before, and she couldn't make it happen again. Then, about a week later, it did: with Mrs Pritchard this time. After her husband had examined the tap and could find nothing wrong with it, he decided that the water supply must be faulty; so they got on to me.

I went round personally, as it was the first complaint

from any of these bungalows. The tap seemed normal, and I remember asking if the schoolboy son could have been experimenting with their main stop, when Mrs Pritchard, who had been fiddling with the tap, suddenly said, 'Quick, look at this! It's off now!' They were quite cocky about its happening when I was there.

It really was odd. I turned the tap to the limit, but—not a drop! Not even the sort of gasping gurgle you hear when the supply is turned off at the main. After a couple of minutes, though, it came on. Water shot out, I should say, with about ten times' normal force, as if it had been held under pressure. Then gradually it died down and ran steadily.

Both children were in the room with us until we all dodged out of the door to escape a soaking—it had splashed all over the ceiling—so they couldn't have been up to any tricks. I promised the Pritchards to have the pipes checked. Before returning to town, I called at the next two bungalows in the row: neither of the tenants had had any trouble at all with the water. I thought, well, that localised it at least.

When I reached my office there was a telephone message waiting from Pritchard. I rang him back and he was obviously annoyed. 'Look here,' he said, 'not ten minutes after you left, we've had something else happen! The wall of the large bedroom's cracked from top to bottom. Big pieces of plaster fell, and the bed's in a terrible mess.' And then he said, 'You wouldn't have got me in a jerry-built place like this if I'd known!'

I had plasterers on the job next morning, and the whole water supply to 'Minuke' under examination. For about three days there was peace. The tap behaved itself, and absolutely nothing was found to be wrong. I was annoyed at what seemed to have been unnecessary expenditure. It looked as if the Pritchards were going to be difficult—and I've had my share of that type: fault-finding cranks occasionally carry eccentricity to the extent of a little private destruction, to prove their points. I was on the watch from now on.

Then it came again.

Pritchard rang me at my home, before nine in the morning. His voice sounded a bit off. Shaky.

'For God's sake can you come round here right away,' he said. 'Tell you about it when you get here.' And then he said, almost fiercely, but quietly and close to the mouthpiece, 'There's something damned queer about this place!' Dramatising is a typical feature of all cranks, I thought, but particularly the little mousy kind, like Pritchard.

I went to 'Minuke' and found that Mrs Pritchard was in bed, in a state of collapse. The doctor had given her a sleeping dose.

Pritchard told me a tale that was chiefly remarkable for the expression on his face as he told it.

I don't know if you're familiar with the layout of that type of bungalow? The living-room is in the front of the house, with the kitchen behind it. To get from one to the other you have to use the little hallway, through two doors. But for convenience at meal-times, there's a serving hatch in the wall between these rooms. A small wooden door slides up and down over the hatch-opening.

'The wife was just passing a big plate of bacon and eggs through from the kitchen,' Pritchard told me, 'when the hatch door came down on her wrists. I saw it and I heard her yell. I thought the cord must've snapped, so I said, "All right, all right!" and went to pull it up because it's only a light wooden frame.'

Pritchard was a funny colour and as far as I could judge, it was genuine.

'Do you know, it wouldn't come! I got my fingers under it and heaved, but it might have weighed two hundredweight. Once it gave an inch or so, and then pressed harder. I said, 'Hold on!' and nipped round through the hall. When I got into the kitchen she was on the floor, fainted. And the hatch-door was hitched up as right as ninepence. That gave me a turn!' He sat down, quite deflated; it didn't appear to be put on. Still, ordinary neurotics can be almost as troublesome as out-and-out cranks.

I tested the hatch, gingerly; and, of course, the cords were sound and it ran easily.

'Possibly a bit stiff at times, being new,' I said. 'They're apt to jam if you're rough with them.' And then, 'By the way, just what were you hinting on the phone?'

He looked at me. It was warm sunlight outside, with a bus passing. Normal enough to take the mike out of Frankenstein's monster. 'Never mind,' he said, and gave a sheepish half-grin. 'Bit of—well, funny construction in this house, though, eh?'

I'm afraid I was rather outspoken with him.

Let alone any twaddle about a month-old bungalow being haunted, I was determined to clamp down on this 'jerry-building' talk. Perhaps I was beginning to have doubts myself.

I wrote straight off to the building company when I'd managed to trace them, busy developing an arterial road about three counties away. I dare say my letter was on the insinuating side: I think I asked if they had any record of difficulties in the construction of this bungalow. At any rate I got a sniffy reply by return, stating that the matter was out of their hands; in addition, their records were not available for discussion. Blind alley.

In the meantime, things at 'Minuke' had worsened to a really frightening degree. I dreaded the phone ringing. One morning the two Pritchards senior awoke to find that nearly all the furniture in their bedroom had been moved about, including the bed they had been sleeping in: they had felt absolutely nothing. Food became suddenly and revoltingly decomposed. All the chimney pots had come down, not just into the garden, but to the far side of the high road, except one which appeared, pulverised, on the living-room floor. The obvious attempts of the Pritchards to keep a rational outlook had put paid to most of my suspicions by this time.

I managed to locate a local man who had been employed during the erection of the bungalows, as an extra hand. He had worked only on the foundations of 'Minuke', but what he had to say was interesting.

They had found the going slow because of striking a layer of enormous flat stones, apparently trimmed slate, but as the site was otherwise excellent, they pressed on, using the stone as foundation where it fitted in with the plan, and laying down rubble where it didn't. The concrete skin over the rubble—my ears burned when I heard about that, I can tell you—this wretched so-called concrete had cracked, or shattered, several times. Which wasn't entirely surprising, if it had been laid as he described. The flat stones, he said had not been seriously disturbed. A workmate had referred to them as a 'giant's grave', so it was possibly an old burial mound. Norse, perhaps—those are fairly common along this coast—or even very much older.

Apart from this—I'm no diehard sceptic, I may as well confess—I was beginning to admit modest theories about a poltergeist, in spite of a lack of corroborative knockings and ornament-throwing. There were two young children in the house, and the lore has it that kids are often unconsciously connected with phenomena of that sort, though usually adolescents. Still, in the real-estate profession you have to be careful, and if I could see the Pritchards safely off the premises without airing these possibilities, it might be kindest to the bungalow's future.

I went to 'Minuke' the same afternoon.

It was certainly turning out an odd nook. I found a

departing policeman on the doorstep. That morning the back door had been burst in by a hundredweight or so of soil, and Mrs Pritchard was trying to convince herself that a practical joker had it in for them. The policeman had taken some notes, and was giving vague advice about 'civil action' which showed that he was out of his depth.

Pritchard looked very tired, almost ill. 'I've got leave from my job, to look after them,' he said, when we were alone. I thought he was wise. He had given his wife's illness as the reason, and I was glad of that.

'I don't believe in—unnatural happenings,' he said.

I agreed with him, non-committally.

'But I'm afraid of what ideas the kids might get. They're both at impressionable ages, y'know.'

I recognised the symptoms without disappointment. 'You mean, you'd rather move elsewhere,' I said.

He nodded. 'I like the district, mind you. But what I—'

There was a report like a gun in the very room.

I found myself with both arms up to cover my face. There were tiny splinters everywhere, and a dust of fibre in the air. The door had exploded. Literally.

To hark back to constructional details, it was one of those light, hollow frame-and-plywood jobs. As you'll know, it takes considerable force to splinter plywood: well this was in tiny fragments. And the oddest thing was that we had felt no blast effect.

In the next room I heard their dog howling. Pritchard was as stiff as a poker.

'I felt it!' he said. 'I felt this lot coming. I've got to knowing when something's likely to happen. It's all round!' Of course I began to imagine I'd sensed something too, but I doubt if I had really; my shock came with the crash. Mrs Pritchard was in the doorway by this time with the kids behind her. He motioned them out and grabbed my arm.

'The thing is,' he whispered, 'that I can still feel it! Stronger than ever, by God! Look, will you stay at home tonight, in case I need—well, in case things get worse? I can phone you.'

On my way back I called at the town library and managed to get hold of a volume on supernatural possession and whatnot. Yes, I was committed now. But the library didn't specialise in that line, and when I opened the book at home, I found it was very little help. 'Vampires of south-eastern Europe' type of stuff. I came across references to something the jargon called an 'elemental' which I took to be a good deal more vicious and destructive than any poltergeist. A thoroughly nasty form of manifestation, if it existed. Those Norse gravestones were fitting into the picture uncomfortably well; it was fashionable in those days to be buried with all the trimmings, human sacrifice and even more unmentionable attractions.

But I read on. After half a chapter on zombies and Rumanian were-wolves, the whole thing began to seem so fantastic that I turned seriously to working out methods of exploding somebody's door as a practical joke. Even a totally certifiable joker would be likelier than vampires. In no time I'd settled down with a whisky, doodling wiring diagrams and only occasionally—like twinges of conscience—speculating on contacting the psychic investigation people.

When the phone rang I was hardly prepared for it. It was a confused, distant voice, gabbling desperately, but I recognised it as Pritchard. 'For God's sake, don't lose a second! Get here—it's all hell on earth! Can't you hear it? My God, I'm going crazy!' And in the background I thought I was able to hear something. A sort of bubbling, shushing 'wah-wah' noise. Indescribable. But you hear some odd sounds on telephones at any time.

'Yes,' I said, 'I'll come immediately. Why don't you all

leave—' But the line had gone dead.

Probably I've never moved faster. I scrambled out to the car with untied shoes flopping, though I remembered to grab a heavy stick in the hall—whatever use it was to be. I drove like fury, heart belting, straight to 'Minuke' expecting to see heaven knows what.

But everything looked still and normal there. The moon was up and I could see the whole place clearly. Curtained lights in the windows. Not a sound.

I rang. After a moment Pritchard opened the door. He was quiet and seemed almost surprised to see me.

I pushed inside. 'Well?' I said. 'What's happened?'

'Not a thing, so far,' he said. 'That's why I didn't expect—'

I felt suddenly angry. 'Look here,' I said, 'what are you playing at? Seems to me that any hoaxing round here begins a lot nearer home than you'd have me believe!' Then the penny dropped. I saw by the fright in his face that he knew something had gone wrong. That was the most horrible, sickening moment of the whole affair for me.

'Didn't you ring?' I said.

And he shook his head.

I've been in some tight spots. But there was always some concrete actual business in hand to screw the mind safely down to. I suppose panic is when the subconscious breaks loose and everything in your head dashes screaming out. It was only just in time that I found a touch of the concrete and actual. A kiddie's paintbox on the floor, very watery.

'The children,' I said. 'Where are they?'

'Wife's just putting the little 'un to bed. She's been restless tonight; just wouldn't go, crying and difficult. Arthur's in the bathroom. Look here, what's happened?'

I told him, making it as short and matter-of-fact as I could. He turned ghastly.

'Better get them dressed and out of here right away,' I said. 'Make some excuse, not to alarm them.'

He'd gone before I finished speaking.

I smoked hard, trying to build up the idea of 'Hoax! Hoax!' in my mind. After all, it could have been. But I knew it wasn't.

Everything looked cosy and normal. Clock ticking. Fire red and mellow. Half-empty cocoa mug on the table. The sound of the sea from beyond the road. I went through to the kitchen. The dog was there, looking up from its sleeping-basket under the sink. 'Good dog,' I said, and it wriggled its tail.

Pritchard came in from the hall. He jumped when he saw me.

'Getting nervy!' he said. 'They won't be long. I don't know where we can go if we—well, if we have to—to leave tonight—'

'My car's outside,' I told him. 'I'll fix you up. Look here, did you ever "hear things"? Odd noises?' I hadn't told him that part of the telephone call.

He looked at me so oddly, I thought he was going to collapse.

'I don't know,' he said. 'Can you?'

'At this moment?'

I listened.

'No,' I said. 'The clock on the shelf. The sea. Nothing else. No.'

'The sea,' he said, barely whispering. 'But you can't hear the sea in this kitchen!'

He was close to me in an instant. Absolutely terrified. 'Yes, I have heard this before! I think we all have. I said it was the sea: so as not to frighten them. But it isn't! And I recognised it when I came in here just now. That's what made me start. It's getting louder: it does that.'

He was right. Like slow breathing. It seemed to emanate from inside the walls, not at a particular spot, but everywhere. We went into the hall, then the front room; it was the same there. Mixed with it now was a sort of thin crying.

'That's Nellie,' Pritchard said. 'The dog: she always whimpers when it's on—too scared to howl. My God. I've never heard it as loud as this before.'

'Hurry them up, will you!' I almost shouted. He went.

The 'breathing' was ghastly. Slobbering. Stertorous, I think the term is. And faster. Oh, yes, I recognised it. The background music to the phone message. My skin was pure ice.

'Come along!' I yelled. I switched on the little radio to drown the noise. The old National Programme, as it was in those days, for late dance music. Believe it or not, what came through that loud-speaker was the same vile sighing noise, at double the volume. And when I tried to switch it off, it stayed the same.

The whole bungalow was trembling. The Pritchards came running in, she carrying the little girl. 'Get them into the car,' I shouted. We heard glass smashing somewhere.

Above our heads there was an almighty thump. Plaster showered down.

Half-way out of the door the little girl screamed, 'Nellie! Where's Nellie? Nellie, Nellie!'

'The dog,' Pritchard moaned. 'Oh, curse it!' He dragged them outside. I dived for the kitchen, where I'd seen the animal, feeling a lunatic for doing it. Plaster was springing out of the walls in painful showers.

In the kitchen I found water everywhere. One tap was squirting like a fire-hose. The other was missing, water belching across the window from a torn end of pipe.

'Nellie!' I called.

Then I saw the dog. It was lying near the oven, quite stiff. Round its neck was twisted a piece of painted piping with the other tap on the end.

Sheer funk got me then. The ground was moving under me. I bolted down the hall, nearly bumped into Pritchard. I yelled and shoved. I could actually feel the house at my back.

We got outside. The noise was like a dreadful snoring, with rumbles and crashes thrown in. One of the lights went out. 'Nellie's run away,' I said, and we all got in the car, the kids bawling. I started up. People were coming out of the other bungalows—they're pretty far apart and the din was just beginning to make itself felt. Pritchard grumbled, 'We can stop now. Think it'd be safe to go back and grab some of the furniture?' As if he was at a fire; but I don't think he knew what he was doing.

'Daddy—look!' screeched the boy.

We saw it. The chimney of 'Minuke' was going up in a horrible way. In the moonlight it seemed to grow quite slowly, to about sixty feet, like a giant crooked finger. And then—burst. I heard bricks thumping down. Somewhere somebody screamed.

There was a glare like an ungodly great lightning flash. It lasted for a second or so.

Of course, we were dazzled, but I thought I saw the whole of 'Minuke' fall suddenly and instantaneously flat, like a swatted fly. I probably did, because that's what happened, anyway.

There isn't much more to tell.

Nobody was really hurt, and we were able to put down the whole thing to a serious electrical fault. Main fuses had blown throughout the whole district, which helped this theory out. Perhaps it was unfortunate in another respect, because a lot of people changed over to gas.

There wasn't much recognisably left of 'Minuke'. But some of the bits were rather unusual. Knots in pipes for instance—I buried what was left of the dog myself. Wood and brick cleanly sliced. Small quantities of

completely powdered metal. The bath had been squashed flat, like tinfoil. In fact, Pritchard was lucky to land the insurance money for his furniture.

My professional problem, of course, remained. The plot where the wretched place had stood. I managed to persuade the owner it wasn't ideal for building on. Incidentally, lifting those stones might reveal something to somebody some day—but not to me, thank you!

I think my eventual solution showed a touch of wit: I let it very cheaply as a scrap-metal dump.

Well? I know I've never been able to make any sense out of it. I hate telling you all this stuff, because it must make me seem either a simpleton or a charlatan. In so far as there's any circumstantial evidence in looking at the place, you can see it in a moment or two. Here's the coast road—

*

The car pulled up at a bare spot beyond a sparse line of bungalows. The space was marked by a straggling, tufty square of privet bushes. Inside I could see a tangle of rusty iron; springs, a car chassis, oil drums.

'The hedge keeps it from being too unsightly,' said the estate agent, as we crossed to it. 'See—the remains of the gate.'

A few half-rotten slats dangled from an upright. One still bore part of a chrome-plated name. 'MI——' and, a little farther on, 'K'.

'Nothing worth seeing now,' he said. I peered inside. 'Not that there ever was much—Look out!' I felt a violent push. In the same instant something zipped past my head and crashed against the car behind. 'My God!'

'Went right at you!' gasped the agent.

It had shattered a window of the car and gone through the open door opposite. We found it in the road beyond, sizzling on the tarmac. A heavy steel nut, white-hot.

'I don't know about you,' the estate agent said, 'but I'm rather in favour of getting out of here.'

And we did. Quickly.

The Witch's Bone

WILLIAM CROFT DICKINSON

Michael Elliot M.A., LL.D., F.S.A.(Scot.) frowned at the letter which had come from the Honorary Curator of the local museum. It was quite a short letter and quite a simple one; merely asking him if he would allow the Museum to borrow his 'Witch's Bone' for a special exhibition covering Folk Beliefs and Customs. But Michael Elliott found the letter far from welcome. Short and simple as it was, it revived and increased all the fearful troubles of his mind. More than that, dare he now let the 'Bone' pass out of his own keeping—even if only for a little while?

Every day, for the last week, that witch's bone had preoccupied his mind to the exclusion of all else. The witch's bone that brought to an end all his quarrels with Mackenzie Grant. The witch's bone that had possibly given him a revenge far more terrible than anything he had sought or expected. In a fit of anger he had thought only of testing its efficacy, never really believing it would work. And now he knew that the bone had worked only too well. Or had it? Had he indeed compassed Grant's death? All he knew was that Grant had died and that now he found it hard to recover his peace of mind.

Of course, he had only himself to blame. He had shown the bone at the last meeting of their local Antiquarian Society, just after he had acquired it; and, pleased with himself, he had expatiated upon its awful power. Mackenzie Grant had contradicted him—as usual. Grant had always treated his theories with contempt. There was his paper on lake-dwellings, and, after that, his paper on the iron-age forts in the Central

Highlands. Upon both occasions Grant had stood up and pooh-poohed everything he had said. At meetings of the Council, too, the man could be relied upon to speak against everything he proposed. But all that was past history. Grant had poured scorn upon his story of the bone. And now Grant was dead. Yet how unbounded would be the relief to his tortured mind if Grant had been right, and if the story of the bone were 'stuff and nonsense' and nothing more. The very night that Grant had ridiculed his story he had put the bone to the test, directing its malevolent powers against Mackenzie Grant. And Grant had died a horrible death a few hours later. But could it not have been a ghastly coincidence in which the bone had played no part at all?

It was only a short piece of bone—probably sheep-bone—about six inches long, with a narrow ring of black bog-oak tightly encircling it near its centre. He had acquired it during his recent holiday in Sutherland. An old woman had died in a remote glen, and, because she had been reputed to be a witch, and had been feared as such, no one would bear her to burial. The local minister had called upon him, beseeching his help. 'The poor body was no witch at all,' the minister had said. 'She was just old and ill-favoured. I have had a coffin made of about the right size—at any rate it will be large enough—and if you could just drive me to the old body's hut, with the coffin in the rear of your estate-wagon, maybe we could manage to coffin her, and give her a Christian burial.'

A strange request to make of any man! But the minister had won him over, and his reward had been the witch's bone.

They had found it on a shelf in the old woman's hut. The minister had seen it first, and had prodded it gently with his finger. 'So,' he had said softly, 'the witch's bone. I have been told of it. There are those of my people who say that she would utter her curse upon some man or woman, and then would make a wax figure and stick a pin into it. Then they say that if this bone rattled on its shelf, she knew that her curse had taken effect and that the person portrayed in the wax would be seized with pains in that part of the body which corresponded with the place of the pin in the wax. Some have even said that she could kill by sticking her pin in the heart or the head. For the power is in the bone. It can wound or kill any who are cursed by its possessor. And never are they spared.'

He had listened and looked with astonishment until, suddenly, the minister's face had changed and he had cried out: 'But what am I saying to you? There is no Witch of Endor in Sutherland. Indeed there is not. No such devilry is possible. I am not believing one word of it.' And the minister had boldly picked up the bone and had offered it to him. 'Take it with you,' he had said. 'It may interest some of your friends in the south.' And, wondering, he had taken it.

Yes, it had interested some of his friends. But Mackenzie Grant had laughed at him. 'A witch's bone!' he had said, contemptuously. 'Stuff and nonsense. Anyone can see by just looking at it that it's a handle, and nothing more. That ring round its centre simply means that, when it is grasped, two fingers go on one side of the ring, and two fingers on the other. Any boy, flying a kite, grasps a piece of wood in exactly the same way at the end of his string. A witch's bone, indeed. I believe, Elliott, I could persuade you that a handkerchief with a hole in it is a witch's veil to be worn at meetings of her coven. And the hole, of course, would be symbolic, indicative of her lapse from the Christian faith.' And so the man had gone on. Laughing at him before his friends.

He had kept down the anger which had surged within him; but, when he had returned home, and had taken the bone from his pocket, all his pent-up feelings had broken their bounds. He had marched straight into his study and, placing the bone upon a bookshelf near the fireplace, had resolved to prove its power to hurt. Aloud and deliberately he had cursed Mackenzie Grant; but, searching for sealing-wax, could find none. Then he had recalled the photograph of Mackenzie Grant in a recent volume of the Transactions of their Society. He had recalled, too, his aversion to destroying any photograph. To tear up a photograph had always seemed to him to be akin to tearing the living flesh and bones. So much the better. Mackenzie Grant should be torn asunder with a vengeance.

He had ripped the full-page photograph from the book and had deliberately torn it to pieces. In the fury of his task he had, for the moment, forgotten the bone. But, as the torn pieces had multiplied between his hands, suddenly there had come a rattling sound from the nearby shelf. And, at that, his heart had turned to ice. Fearfully he had looked at the bone; it lay exactly where he had placed it, and it lay inert and still. He remembered assuring himself that he had simply imagined that rattle. He was overwrought. Yes, it was imagination and nothing more.

Yet, the next morning, when reading the *Scotsman* at breakfast-time, again a chill had struck his heart and his whole body had numbed with fear. For the paper announced with regret that a distinguished antiquary, Mr Mackenzie Grant, had been killed in a road accident. According to the announcement, Mr Grant, when driving home about midnight, after having dined with a friend, had unaccountably run head-on into a heavy lorry that had stopped for some minor adjustment on the opposite side of the road. It was a bad accident. Grant's car has been completely telescoped. But, in the opinion of the doctors, he must have been killed instantaneously, for their examination showed that he had suffered multiple injuries and that practically every bone in his body was broken.

No wonder his mind was ill at ease. He had striven to persuade himself that it was pure coincidence. That those multiple injuries had naught to do with a photograph torn into many shreds. He had laboured to free himself from a haunting burden of guilt. Yet the torturing thought was still there. Had the bone indeed the power of killing those who were cursed by its possessor?

Since then he had locked it up in his coin-cabinet. He had even been afraid to open the cabinet to make certain it was still there. And now the Museum had asked to be allowed to borrow it, to put it on display. To say that he had lost it, or had destroyed it, would be childish. Yet dare he lend it? Dare he allow it to pass out of his own keeping?

These were but some of the thoughts that troubled the mind of Dr Michael Elliott as he sat with a letter that lay before him on his desk.

*

About nine o'clock in the evening of the same day, when Sir Stephen Rowandson C.I.E. the Honorary Curator of the Museum, was deep in a detective story, his housekeeper knocked on his study door and announced: 'Dr Michael Elliott.'

Somewhat surprised, Rowandson put down his book and rose to greet his visitor.

'Come in, Elliott. Come in. This is an unexpected pleasure.'

Michael Elliott entered the room slowly and hesitantly.

'Man, but you do look tired,' continued Rowandson, as Elliott came into the light. 'It's these cold nights. Take that chair by the fire and warm yourself. I'll get you a whisky.'

Elliott took the proffered chair and sank down in it. If, indeed, he was looking tired, he knew full well that it was not due to the coldness of the night.

'I've called about your letter, asking for the loan of my witch's bone,' he said, turning to his host and gratefully accepting the whisky which had been poured out for him. 'I thought I'd sooner bring it to you personally at your home, rather than give it to you, or leave it for you, at the Museum.'

'Why, certainly,' replied Rowandson, concealing his surprise. 'You think I might possibly leave it lying about in the Museum, and it might fall into the wrong hands?'

Rowandson spoke with a smile, But Elliott coloured slightly.

'You have guessed correctly. It may be more dangerous than we know.'

Rowandson looked more closely at his visitor. Did Elliott really believe that this bit of bone could exert occult force? He had been one of those standing by when Mackenzie Grant had poured scorn upon it; and although he had not heard Elliott's account of its supposed malignant power, he knew full well that the man was apt to be too credulous. But perhaps he had better humour him.

'You are right,' he conceded, gravely. 'I have seen some strange things myself in India. We must be careful. Would it make you happier if I promised that when I do put it on display I will put it in a locked case?'

Elliott's relief was too apparent to be disguised.

'I was hoping for something like that,' he said, taking the bone from his breast pocket. 'It is good of you to go to so much trouble; but I should feel reassured if it was under lock and key.'

'You can rely on me,' returned Rowandson, 'I will keep it safely here, in the house, until I have a locked case ready for it. And I will tell no one it is here.'

Once more Elliott's relief was so obvious that Rowandson, taking the bone from him, ostentatiously looked around his study for a safe keeping-place. Not finding one, he placed the bone on his desk. 'I'll find a safe place for it later,' he assured Elliott. 'You can rely on me. And I will certainly keep it here until I take it personally to the Museum and myself place it in a display case that can be securely locked.'

Thereafter for some ten minutes or so, Sir Stephen Rowandson strove in vain to find some topic of conversation which would interest his visitor. But Elliott answered only in monosyllables, while his eyes constantly strayed to the witch's bone lying on the Curator's desk, and his only thought was whether he should warn Rowandson of its dangerous power, or whether that would merely make him look foolish and at the same time make Rowandson less responsive and also more careless.

'Well,' said Rowandson, as he wearied of his task, 'I mustn't keep you too late. And don't worry about your bone. It will be quite safe.'

Elliott rose heavily to his feet. 'Thank you,' he said. 'I am sorry to be so fussy, but, you know, I do believe it may be a witch's bone and not, as . . . as . . . Mackenzie Grant maintained, simply a handle of some kind.'

The last words had come out with difficulty, and Rowandson thought he understood.

'Yes, poor fellow. We shall miss his sceptical comments. We were all his victims at one time or another.'

Elliott winced. Again his eyes strayed to the witch's bone.

'You won't leave it there, will you?' he asked.

'No, no,' replied Rowandson, quickly, 'I'll find a safe place for it all right.'

Seemingly reassured, Elliott moved towards the door of the room. Rowandson opened it and, conducting his visitor through the hall, let him out of the house. For a minute or two he watched the retreating figure. 'There goes one of the most distinguished classical scholars in Europe,' he said to himself, 'and yet with more antiquarian bees in his bonnet than any man I know. A witch's bone, indeed. It may be. But, even so, what harm can it do to anyone?'

He returned to his study and, picking up the bone from his desk, examined it under the reading lamp. But his examination made him no wiser.

'Well, well. Old Elliott was certainly mighty concerned about it, and I'd better do what I said. But where shall I put the wretched thing? I haven't a safe, and there isn't a drawer in the whole house that would defeat a ten-year-old.'

Moving about the room with the bone in his hand, Rowandson finally stopped in front of an old-fashioned knick-knack stand which bore on its shelves a medley of flints, cylindrical seals, Roman nails, and other small archaeological objects of varying periods and kinds. 'The very place,' he muttered. 'Not so much Poe's idea in "The Purloined Letter" as Chesterton's idea of hiding a leaf in a forest.'

By moving some of the specimens closer to one another he cleared a small space on one of the shelves and placed the bone there. Stepping back, he surveyed the result and found it good.

*

Two days later, as Sir Stephen Rowandson entered his study after a frugal breakfast, he was feeling thoroughly disgruntled. His housekeeper, summoned yesterday afternoon to nurse a sister who had suddenly been taken ill, had left him to fend for himself; and Sir Stephen Rowandson was not accustomed to domestic work. He had managed to prepare his coffee, toast and marmalade for breakfast; but now the dead ashes in his study fire-place mocked him. He would have to take out those ashes and lay the fire himself. Unwillingly he began his task. As he busied himself with paper and firewood, his mind turned to the Museum and to his forthcoming exhibition. And his thoughts made him more disgruntled still. Why should everything go wrong at one and the same time? For, yesterday morning, when one or two members of the Society had come to the Museum to help with the final preparations, and when, in accordance with his promise, he had arranged for a place in one of the two locked cases to be reserved for Michael Elliott's witch's bone, the interfering and officious Colonel Hogan had actually presumed to give contrary orders, even asserting that the bone wasn't worth a place in the exhibition anywhere. He had had trouble with the Colonel before. The man seemed to think he was in command of everything. But this time there had followed an unseemly wrangle in which he had completely lost his temper. More than that, in defending his promise to Elliott, he had hotly argued that the bone might be more dangerous than any of them realised. That heated altercation had made him look foolish; and he remembered, to his annoyance, the glances that had been exchanged. The word would now go round that he was becoming as credulous as Elliott himself. But if Elliott hadn't been so fussy, the argument would never have started at all.

'I could curse the old fool,' he muttered angrily, as he thrust the sticks of firewood among the paper which he had crushed up and laid in the hearth. 'Damn Michael Elliott, and damn his bone.'

He finished laying the fire and rose up from his task when, as he did so, he heard a strange rattle which seemed to come from somewhere within the room. Startled, he looked round. But nothing had fallen; nothing seemed to be out of place. 'Probably a bird fluttered against the window,' he said dubiously. 'But it didn't sound like it. It was a queer sound. Never heard

anything like it before.'

Well, what now? He could go to the Museum and work there, then he could lunch at his Club; back to the Museum again; dinner at the Club; and perhaps he could even collect together a bridge-four for the evening. Yes, he could manage without his housekeeper for a day or two. But he hoped it wouldn't be longer than that.

*

Everything had worked according to plan, and Sir Stephen Rowandson was feeling much happier. He had put in a good morning's work; he had had an excellent lunch at his Club—and had even arranged a bridge-four; he had carried on with his exhibition in the afternoon; and, to his great relief, the members who had dropped in to help had given no indication that yesterday's wrangle had affected them in any way at all. It was nearly five o'clock, and he was thinking of giving up for the day, when he heard the bell ring. That was unusual. Who could be ringing the bell? The door was open, and people just walked in. Somewhat puzzled, he went to the door and found there a young man.

'Sir Stephen Rowandson?'

'Yes.'

'My name is Robert Reid, sir. You won't know me, but I'm the local representative of the *Scotsman* and I was told you might be able to help me.'

Sir Stephen Rowandson led his visitor into the main room of the Museum.

'And what can I do to help you?' he asked.

'I'm anxious to trace a photograph of Dr Michael Elliott. The paper wishes to carry one tomorrow. I do not like to call at his house, and it was suggested to me that probably you would have one here since, or so I gather, Dr Elliott was a prominent member of your Society.'

'But why can't you call at his house?'

The young man looked up quickly.

'But, of course, how stupid of me. You cannot have heard.' Then in a slightly lower voice, he continued: 'I'm very sorry to tell you, sir, that Dr Michael Elliott is dead. He was killed in a bad accident in Edinburgh, about half-past eleven this morning. And, as you will understand, we must carry a fairly long obituary notice. We would also like a photograph, if possible.'

'Michael Elliott dead,' repeated Rowandson, dully.

'Yes, sir. Apparently he was walking along the pavement by a site where a new building is going up when, for some unknown reason, a steel girder that was being lifted by a crane slipped from the chains which were holding it. Hitting the side of the building, it slewed round and, by sheer bad luck, fell on Dr Elliott and crushed him to death.'

'How horrible!'

'Yes, sir. But we are told that death must have been instantaneous. For not only was Dr Elliott badly crushed but also the girder, in falling, broke down a wooden screen which was shielding the site, and, according to the doctors, drove a wedge of broken wood from the screen straight through Dr Elliott's heart.'

For a brief space, Sir Stephen Rowardson remained silent.

'It comes to all of us, sooner or later,' he said at last. 'But I wish it could have come in a way different from this. A photograph? Yes, I think I can help. There was a photograph of Dr Elliott in our local paper, the *Standard*, only the other day. Come up to my house and I'll show it to you. Then, if you think it suitable, I'm sure the *Standard* people will be only too glad to lend you the block.'

*

Sir Stephen Rowandson led the newspaper-man into his study, where, almost at once, he apologised for the coldness of the room.

'I'm sorry to offer you such a chilly reception,' he said. 'But my housekeeper is away and I am looking after myself. However, we'll soon have a fire, and then I'll hunt for that photograph.'

Although the young man held out a restraining hand, Rowandson struck a match, and lit the fire. Then, crossing to a pile of newspapers on a small table by his desk, he began to turn over the papers one by one. But the *Standard* which he wanted was not there.

'Queer,' he said, 'I could have sworn it was in this pile. But warm yourself at what fire there is while

I have a look in the dining-room. I sometimes leave the paper there.'

He went out of the room, and the young man looked ruefully at the fire. The edges of the paper had burned, but nothing more. As one last wisp of smoke curled up towards the chimney, the fire was out.

'I can't find it anywhere,' growled Rowandson, coming back into the room. Once more he went through the pile of papers on the table, and still without success. Then he saw the dead hearth.

'Oh, I am sorry,' he cried. 'The fire has gone out. I must have packed it too tightly. Stupid of me. But it's years since I laid a fire.'

Then a new thought came to him.

'And I'm willing to bet that the *Standard* I'm looking for is there, at the bottom of my wretched fire. I just took the first paper that came to hand. I really am sorry. But look! If you go to the offices of the *Standard*, in the High Street, they'll willingly show you the issue, and then you can ask about the block. Say I sent you. Really, I should have taken you there in the first place.'

With many apologies for troubling the Honorary Curator of the Museum, the young newspaper-man left. Sir Stephen Rowandson returned to his study and there looked balefully at the dead fire.

'I suppose I shall have to re-lay the damned thing,' he muttered to himself. 'I'd better do it now, and have done with it.'

Kneeling down in front of the hearth, he removed the coal, then the firewood, and finally the paper. Yes, he had packed it too tightly. But he had learned his lesson. Straightening out a piece of the crushed-up paper, he saw it was the *Standard* for which he had been looking. He might have guessed he would use the one newspaper that was wanted. Ah! here was the page that bore poor Elliott's photograph. He straightened the page. It was still a good likeness, even though the photograph was badly crushed, and a splinter from the rough firewood had pierced it in the very heart.

But all that held no significance for Sir Stephen Rowandson. He re-laid the fire, went to his bathroom, and there—washed his hands.

Lucky's Grove

H. R. WAKEFIELD

Mr Braxton strolled with his land-agent, Curtis, into the Great Barn.

'There you are,' said Curtis in a satisfied tone, 'the finest little larch I ever saw, and the kiddies will never set eyes on a lovelier Christmas tree.'

Mr Braxton examined it; it stood twenty feet from huge green pot to crisp, straight peak, and was exquisitely sturdy, fresh and symmetrical.

'Yes, it's a beauty,' he agreed. 'Where did you find it?'

'In that odd little spinney they call Lucky's Grove in the long meadow near the river boundary.'

'Oh!' remarked Mr Braxton uncertainly. To himself he was saying vaguely, 'He shouldn't have got it from there, of course he wouldn't realise it, but he shouldn't have got it from there.'

'Of course we'll replant it,' said Curtis, noticing his employer's diminished enthusiasm. 'It's a curious thing, but it isn't a young tree; it's apparently full-grown. Must be a dwarf variety, but I don't know as much about trees as I should like.'

Mr Braxton was surprised to find there was one branch of country lore on which Curtis was not an expert; for he was about the best known man at his job in the British Isles. Pigs, bees, chickens, cattle, crops, running a shoot, he had mastered them one and all. He paid him two thousand a year with house and car. He was worth treble.

'I expert it's all right,' said Mr Braxton, 'it's just that Lucky's Grove is—is—well, "sacred" is perhaps too strong a word. Maybe I should have told you, but

I expect it's all right.'

'That accounts for it then,' laughed Curtis. 'I thought there seemed some reluctance on the part of the men while we were yanking it up and getting it on the lorry. They handled it a bit gingerly; on the part of the older men, I mean; the youngsters didn't worry.'

'Yes, there would be,' said Mr Braxton. 'But never mind, it'll be back in a few days and it's a superb little tree. I'll bring Mrs Braxton along to see it after lunch,' and he strolled back into Abingdale Hall.

Fifty-five years ago Mr Braxton's father had been a labourer on this very estate, and in that year young Percy, aged eight, had got an errand boy's job in Oxford. Twenty years later he'd owned one small shop. Twenty-five years after that fifty big shops. Now, though he had finally retired, he owned two hundred and eighty vast shops and was a millionaire whichever way you added it up. How had this happened? No one can quite answer such questions. Certainly he'd worked like a brigade of Trojans, but midnight oil has to burn in Aladdin's Lamp before it can transform ninepence into one million pounds. It was just that he asked no quarter from the unforgiving minute, but squeezed from it the fruit of others' many hours. Those like Mr Braxton seem to have their own time-scale; they just say the word and up springs a fine castle of commerce, but the knowledge of that word cannot be imported; it is as mysterious as the Logos. But all through his great labours he had been moved by one fixed resolve—to avenge his father—that fettered spirit—for he had been an able, intelligent man who had had no earthly chance of revealing the fact to the world. Always the categorical determination had blazed in his son's brain, 'I will own Abingdale Hall, and, where my father sweated, I will rule and be lord.' And of course it had happened. Fate accepts the dictates of such men as Mr Braxton, shrugs its shoulders, and leaves its revenge to

Death. The Hall had come on the market just when he was about to retire, and with an odd delight, an obscure sense of home-coming, the native returned, and his riding-boots, shooting-boots, golf shoes, and all the many glittering guineas' worth, stamped in and obliterated the prints of his father's hob-nails.

That was the picture he often re-visualised, the way it amused him to 'put it to himself,' as he roamed his broad acres and surveyed the many glowing triumphs of his model husbandry.

Some credit was due to buxom, blithe and debonair Mrs Braxton, kindly, competent and innately adaptable. She was awaiting him in the morning room and they went in solitary state, to luncheon. But it was the last peaceful lunch they would have for a spell—the 'Families' were pouring in on the morrow.

As a footman was helping them to *Sole Meunière*, Mr Braxton said, 'Curtis has found a very fine Christmas tree. It's in the barn. You must come and look at it after lunch.'

'That *is* good,' replied his wife. 'Where did he get it from?'

Mr Braxton hesitated for a moment.

'From Lucky's Grove.'

Mrs Braxton looked up sharply.

'From the grove!' she said, surprised.

'Yes, of course he didn't realise—anyway it'll be all right, it's all rather ridiculous, and it'll be replanted before the New Year.'

'Oh, yes,' agreed Mrs Braxton. 'After all it's only just a clump of trees.'

'Quite. And it's just the right height for the ballroom. It'll be taken in there tomorrow morning and the electricians will work on it in the afternoon.'

'I heard from Lady Pounser just now,' said Mrs Braxton. 'She's bringing six over, that'll make seventy-four; only two refusals. The presents are arriving this afternoon.'

They discussed the party discursively over the cutlets and Peach Melba and soon after lunch walked across to the barn. Mr Braxton waved to Curtis, who was examining a new tractor in the garage fifty yards away, and he came over.

Mrs Braxton looked the tree over and was graciously delighted with it, but remarked that the pot could have done with another coat of paint. She pointed to several streaks, rust-coloured, running through the green. 'Of course it won't show when it's wrapped, but they didn't do a very good job.'

Curtis leant down. 'They certainly didn't,' he answered irritably. 'I'll see to it. I think it's spilled over from the soil: that copse is on a curious patch of red sand—there are some at Frilford too. When we pulled it up I noticed that the roots were stained a dark crimson.' He put his hand down and scraped at the stains with his thumb. He seemed a shade puzzled.

'It shall have another coat at once,' he said. 'What did you think of Lampson and Collett's scheme for the barn?'

'Quite good,' replied Mrs Braxton, 'but the sketches for the chains are too fancy.'

'I agree,' said Curtis, who usually did so in the case of un-essentials, reserving his tactful vetoes for the others.

The Great Barn was by far the most aesthetically satisfying, as it was the oldest feature of the Hall buildings; it was vast, exquisitely proportioned, and mellow. That could hardly be said of the house itself, which the 4th Baron of Abingdale had rebuilt on the cinders of its predecessor in 1752.

This nobleman had travelled abroad extensively and returned with most enthusiastic, grandiose and indigestible ideas of architecture. The result was a gargantuan piece of rococo-jocoso which only an entirely humourless pedant could condemn. It contained forty-two bedrooms and eighteen reception rooms—so Mrs Braxton had made it at the last recount. But Mr Braxton had not repeated with the interior the errors of the 4th Baron. He'd briefed the greatest expert in Europe with the result that the interior was quite tasteful and sublimely comfortable.

'Ugh!' he exclaimed, as they stepped out into the air. 'It *is* getting nippy!'

'Yes,' said Curtis, 'there's a nor-'easter blowing up—may be snow for Christmas.'

On getting back to the house Mrs Braxton went into a huddle with butler and housekeeper, and Mr Braxton retired to his study for a doze. But instead his mind settled on Lucky's Grove. When he'd first seen it again after buying the estate, it seemed as if fifty years had rolled away, and he realised that Abingdale was far more summed up to him in the little copse than in the gigantic barracks two miles away. At once he felt at home again. Yet, just as when he'd been a small boy, the emotion the Grove had aroused in him had been sharply tinged with awe, so it had been now, half a century later. He still had a sneaking dread of it. How precisely he could see it, glowing darkly in the womb of the fire before him, standing starkly there in the centre of the big, fallow field, a perfect circle; and first, a ring of holm-oaks and, facing east, a breach therein to the larches and past them on the west a gap to the yews. It had always required a tug at his courage—not always forthcoming—to pass through them and face the mighty Scotch fir, rearing up its great bole from the grass mound. And when he stood before it, he'd always known an odd longing to fling himself down and—well, worship—it was the only word—the towering tree. His father had told him his forebears had done that very thing, but always when alone and at certain seasons of the year; and that no bird or beast was ever seen there. A lot of traditional nonsense, no doubt, but he himself had absorbed the spirit of the place and knew it would always be so.

One afternoon in late November, a few weeks after they had moved in, he'd gone off alone in the drowsing misty dusk; and when he'd reached the holm-oak bastion and seen the giant tree surrounded by its sentinels, he'd known again that quick turmoil of confused emotions. As he'd walked slowly towards it, it had seemed to quicken and be aware of his coming. As he passed the shallow grassy fosse and entered the oak ring he felt there was something he ought to say, some greeting, password or prayer. It was the most aloof, silent little place under the sun, and oh, so old. He'd tiptoed past the larches and faced the barrier of yews. He'd stood there for a long musing minute, tingling with the sensation that he was being watched and regarded. At length he stepped forward and stood before the God—that mighty word came abruptly and unforeseen—and he felt a wild desire to fling himself down on the mound and do obeisance. And then he'd hurried home. As he recalled all this most vividly and minutely, he was seized with a sudden gust of uncontrollable anger at the thought of the desecration of the grove. He knew now that if he'd had the slightest idea of Curtis's purpose he'd have resisted and opposed it. It was too late now. He realised he'd 'worked himself up' rather absurdly. What could it matter! He was still a superstitious bumpkin at heart. Anyway it was no fault of Curtis. It was the finest Christmas tree anyone could hope for, and the whole thing was too nonsensical for words. The general tone of these cadentic conclusions did not quite accurately represent his thoughts—a very rare failing with Mr Braxton.

About dinner-time the blizzard set furiously in, and

the snow was lying.

'Chains on the cars tomorrow,' Mrs Braxton told the head chauffeur.

'Boar's Hill'll be a beggar,' thought that person.

Mr and Mrs Braxton dined early, casually examined the presents and went to bed. Mr Braxton was asleep at once as usual, but was awakened by the beating of a blind which had slipped its moorings. Reluctantly he got out of bed and went to fix it. As he was doing so he became conscious of the frenzied hysterical barking of a dog. The sound, muffled by the gale, came, he judged, from the barn. He believed the underkeeper kept his whippet there. Scared by the storm, he supposed, and returned to bed.

The morning was brilliantly fine and cold, but the snowfall had been heavy.

'I heard a dog howling in the night, Perkins,' said Mr Braxton to the butler at breakfast; 'Drake's I imagine. What's the matter with it?'

'I will ascertain, sir,' said Perkins.

'It *was* Drake's dog,' he announced a little later. 'Apparently something alarmed the animal, for when Drake went to let it out this morning, it appeared to be extremely frightened. When the barn door was opened, it took to its heels and, although Drake pursued it, it jumped into the river and Drake fears it was drowned.'

'Um,' said Mr Braxton, 'must have been the storm; whippets are nervous dogs.'

'So I understand, sir.'

'Drake was so fond of it,' said Mrs Braxton, 'though it always looked so naked and shivering to me.'

'Yes, madam,' agreed Perkins, 'it had that appearance.'

Soon after, Mr Braxton sauntered out into the blinding glitter. Curtis came over from the garage. He was heavily muffled up.

'They've got chains on all the cars,' he said. 'Very seasonable and all that, but farmers have another word for it.' His voice was thick and hoarse.

'Yes,' said Mr Braxton. 'You're not looking very fit.'

'Not feeling it. Had to get up in the night. Thought I heard someone trying to break into the house: thought I saw him too.'

'Indeed,' said Mr Braxton. 'Did you see what he was like?'

'No,' replied Curtis uncertainly. 'It was snowing like the devil. Anyway, I got properly chilled to the marrow, skipping around in my nightie.'

'You'd better get to bed,' said Mr Braxton solicitously. He had affection and a great respect for Curtis.

'I'll stick it out today and see how I feel tomorrow. We're going to get the tree across in a few minutes. Can I borrow the two footmen? I want another couple of pullers and haulers.'

Mr Braxton consented, and went off on his favourite little stroll across the sparkling meadows to the river and the pool where the big trout set their running noses to the stream.

Half an hour later Curtis had mobilised his scratch team of sleeve-rolled assistants and, with Perkins steering and himself braking, they got to grips with the tree and bore it like a camouflaged battering-ram towards the ballroom, which occupied the left centre of the frenetic frontage on the ground floor. There was a good deal of bumping and boring and genial blasphemy before the tree was manoeuvred into the middle of the room and levered by rope and muscle into position. As it came up its pinnacle just cleared the ceiling. Sam, a cow-man, whose ginger mop had been buried in the foliage for some time, exclaimed tartly as he slapped the trunk, 'There ye are, ye old sod! Thanks for the scratches on me mug, ye old—!'

The next thing he was lying on his back, a livid weal across his right cheek.

This caused general merriment and even Perkins permitted himself a spectral smile. There was more astonishment than pain on the face of Sam. He stared at the tree in a humble way for a moment, like a chastised and guilty dog, and then slunk from the room. The merriment of the others died away.

'More spring in these branches than you'd think,' said Curtis to Perkins.

'No doubt, sir, that is due to the abrupt release of the tension,' replied Perkins scientifically.

The 'Families' met at Paddington and travelled down together, so at five o'clock three car-loads drew up at the Hall. There were Jack and Mary with Paddy aged eight, Walter and Pamela with Jane and Peter, seven and five respectively, and George and Gloria with Gregory and Phyllis, ten and eight.

Jack and Walter were sons of the house. They were much of a muchness, burly, handsome and as dominating as their sire; a fine pair of commercial kings, entirely capable rulers, but just lacking that something which founds dynasties. Their wives conformed equally to the social type to which they belonged, good-lookers, smart dressers, excellent wives and mothers; but rather coolly colourless, spiritually. Their offspring were 'charming children,' flawless products of the English matrix, though Paddy showed signs of some obstreperous originality. 'George' was the Honourable George Calvin Roderick etcetera Penables, and Gloria was Mr and Mrs Braxton's only daughter. George had inherited half a million and had started off at twenty-four to be something big in the city. In a sense he achieved his ambition, for two years later he was generally reckoned the biggest 'something' in the City, from which he then withdrew, desperately clutching his last hundred thousand and vowing lachrymose repentance. He had kept his word and his wad, hunted and shot six days a week in winter, and spent most of the summer wrestling with the two dozen devils in his golf bag. According to current jargon he was the complete extrovert, but what a relief are such, in spite of the pitying shrugs of those who for ever are peering into the septic recesses of their souls.

Gloria had inherited some of her father's force. She was rather overwhelmingly primed with energy and pep for her opportunities of releasing it. So she was always rather pent up and explosive, though maternity had kept the pressure down. She was dispassionately fond of George who had presented her with a nice little title and aristocratic background and two 'charming children.' Phyllis gave promise of such extreme beauty that, beyond being the cynosure of every press-camera's eye, and making a resounding match, no more was to be expected of her. Gregory, however, on the strength of some aristic precocity and a violent temper was already somewhat prematurely marked down as a genius to be.

Such were the 'Families.'

During the afternoon four engineers arrived from one of the Braxton factories to fix up the lighting of the tree. The fairy lamps for this had been specially designed and executed for the occasion. Disney figures had been grafted upon them and made to revolve by an ingenious mechanism; the effect being to give the tree, when illuminated, an aspect of whirling life meant to be very cheerful and pleasing.

Mr Braxton happened to see these electricians departing in their lorry and noticed one of them had a bandaged arm and a rather white face. He asked Perkins what had happened.

'A slight accident, sir. A bulb burst and burnt him in some manner. But the injury is, I understand, not of a very serious nature.'

'He looked a bit white.'

'Apparently, sir, he got a fright, a shock of some kind, when the bulb exploded.'

After dinner the grown-ups went to the ballroom. Mr Braxton switched on the mechanism and great enthusiasm was shown. 'Won't the kiddies love it,' said George, grinning at the kaleidoscope. 'Look at the Big Bad Wolf. He looks so darn realistic I'm not sure I'd give him a "U" certificate.'

'It's almost frightening,' said Pamela, 'they look incredibly real. Daddy, you really are rather bright, darling.'

It was arranged that the work of decoration should be tackled on the morrow and finished on Christmas Eve.

'All the presents have arrived,' said Mrs Braxton, 'and are being unpacked. But I'll explain about them tomorrow.'

They went back to the drawing-room. Presently Gloria puffed and remarked: 'Papa, aren't you keeping the house rather too hot?'

'I noticed the same thing,' said Mrs Braxton.

Mr Braxton walked over to a thermometer on the wall. 'You're right,' he remarked, 'seventy.' He rang the bell.

'Perkins,' he asked, 'who's on the furnace?'

'Churchill, sir.'

'Well, he's overdoing it. It's seventy. Tell him to get it back to fifty-seven.'

Perkins departed and returned shortly after.

'Churchill informs me he has damped down and cannot account for the increasing warmth, sir.'

'Tell him to get it back to fifty-seven at once,' rapped Mr Braxton.

'Very good, sir.'

'Open a window,' said Mrs Braxton.

'It is snowing again, madam.'

'My God!' exclaimed Mary, when she and Jack went up to bed. 'That furnace-man is certainly stepping on it. Open all the windows.'

A wild flurry of snow beat against the curtains.

Mr Braxton did what he very seldom did, woke up in the early hours. He awoke sweating from a furtive and demoralising dream. It had seemed to him that he had been crouching down in the fosse round Lucky's Grove, and peering beneath the holm-oaks and that there had been activity of a sort vaguely to be discerned therein, some quick shadowy business. He knew a very tight terror at the thought of being detected at this spying, but he could not wrench himself away. That was all, and he awoke still trembling and troubled. No wonder he'd had such a nightmare, the room seemed like a stokehold. He went to the windows and flung another open, and as he did so he glanced out. His room looked over the rock garden and down the path to the maze. Something moving just outside it caught his eye. He thought he knew what it was, that big Alsatian which had been sheep-worrying in the neighbourhood. What an enormous brute! Or was it just because it was outlined against the snow? It vanished suddenly, apparently into the maze. He'd organise a hunt for it after Christmas; if the snow lay, it should be easy to track.

The first thing he did after breakfast was to send for Churchill, severely reprimand him and threaten him with dismissal from his ship. That person was almost tearfully insistent that he had obeyed orders and kept his jets low. 'I can't make it out, sir. It's got no right to be as 'ot as what it is.'

'That's nonsense!' said Mr Braxton. 'The system has been perfected and cannot take charge, as you suggest. See to it. You don't want me to get an engineer down, do you?'

'No, sir.'

'That's enough. Get it to fifty-seven and keep it there.'

Shortly after, Mrs Curtis rang up to say her husband was quite ill with a temperature and that the doctor was coming. Mr Braxton asked her to ring him again after he'd been.

During the morning the children played in the snow. After a pitched battle in which the girls lost their tempers, Gregory organised the erection of a snow-man. He designed, the others fetched the material. He knew he had a reputation for brilliance to maintain and he produced something Epsteinish, huge and squat. The other children regarded it with little enthusiasm, but, being Gregory, they supposed it must be admired. When it was finished, Gregory wandered off by himself while the others went in to dry. He came in a little late for lunch, during which he was silent and pre-occupied. Afterwards the grown-ups sallied forth.

'Let's see your snow-man, Greg,' said Gloria, in a mother-of-genius tone.

'It isn't all his, we helped,' said Phyllis, voicing a point of view which was to have many echoes in the coming years.

'Why, he's changed it!' exclaimed a chorus two minutes later.

'What an ugly thing!' exclaimed Mary, rather pleased at being able to say so with conviction.

Gregory had certainly given his imagination its head, for now the squat, inert trunk was topped by a big wolf's head with open jaw and ears snarlingly laid back, surprisingly well modelled. Trailing behind it was a coiled, serpentine tail.

'Whatever gave you the idea for that?' asked Jack.

Usually Gregory was facile and eloquent in explaining his inspiration, but this time he refused to be drawn, bit his lip and turned away.

There was a moment's silence and then Gloria said with convincing emphasis, 'I think it's wonderful, Greg!'

And then they all strolled off to examine the pigs and the poultry and the Suffolk Punches.

They had just got back for tea when the telephone

rang in Mr Braxton's study. It was Mrs Curtis. The patient was no better and Doctor Knowles had seemed rather worried, and so on. So Mr Braxton rang up the doctor.

'I haven't diagnosed his trouble, yet,' he said. 'And I'm going to watch him carefully and take a blood-test if he's not better tomorrow. He has a temperature of a hundred and two, but no other superficial symptoms, which is rather peculiar. By the way, one of your cowmen, Sam Colley, got a nasty wound on the face yesterday and shows signs of blood poisoning. I'm considering sending him to hospital. Some of your other men have been in to see me—quite a little outbreak of illness since Tuesday. However, I hope we'll have a clean bill again soon. I'll keep you informed about Curtis.'

Mr Braxton was one of those incredible people who never have a day's illness—till their first and last. Consequently his conception of disease was unimaginative and mechanical. If one of his more essential human machines was running unsatisfactorily, there was a machine-mender called a doctor whose business it was to ensure that all the plug leads were attached firmly and that the manifold drain-pipe was not blocked. But he found himself beginning to worry about Curtis, and this little epidemic amongst his henchmen affected him disagreeably—there was something disturbing to his spirit about it. But just what and why, he couldn't analyse and decide.

After dinner, with the children out of the way, the business of decorating the tree was begun. The general scheme had been sketched out and coloured by one of the Braxton display experts and the company consulted this as they worked, which they did rather silently; possibly, Mr Braxton's palpable anxiety somewhat affected them.

Pamela stayed behind after the others had left the ballroom to put some finishing touches to her section of the tree. When she rejoined the others she was looking rather white and tight-lipped. She said good-night a shade abruptly and went to her room. Walter, a very, very good husband, quickly joined her.

'Anything the matter, old girl?' he asked anxiously.

'Yes,' replied Pamela, 'I'm frightened.'

'Frightened! What d'you mean?'

'You'll think it's all rot, but I'll tell you. When you'd all left the ballroom, I suddenly felt very uneasy—you know the sort of feeling when one keeps on looking round and can't concentrate. However, I stuck at it. I was a little way up the steps when I heard a sharp hiss from above me in the tree. I jumped back to the floor and looked up; now, of course you won't believe me, but the trunk of the tree was moving—it was like the coils of a snake writhing upwards, and there was something at the top of the tree, horrid-looking, peering at me. I know you won't believe me.'

Walter didn't, but he also didn't know what to make of it. 'I know what happened!' he improvised lightly. 'You'd been staring in at that trunk for nearly two hours and you got dizzy—like staring at the sun on the sea; and that snow dazzle this afternoon helped it. You've heard of snow-blindness—something like that, it still echoes from the retina or whatever . . .'

'You think it might have been that?'

'I'm sure of it.'

'And that horrible head?'

'Well, as George put it rather brightly, I don't think some of those figures on the lamps should get a "U" certificate. There's the wolf to which he referred, and the witch.'

'Which witch?' laughed Pamela a little hysterically. 'I didn't notice one.'

'I did. I was working just near it, at least, I supppose it's meant to be a witch. A figure in black squinting from behind a tree. As a matter of fact fairies never seemed all fun and frolic to me, there's often something diabolical about them—or rather casually cruel. Disney knows that.'

'Yes, there is,' agreed Pamela. 'So you think that's all there was to it?'

'I'm certain. One's eyes can play tricks on one.'

'Yes,' said Pamela. 'I know what you mean, as if they saw what one knew wasn't there or was different. Though who would "one" be then?'

'Oh, don't ask me that sort of question!' laughed Walter. 'Probably Master Gregory will be able to tell you in a year or two.'

'He's a nice little boy, really,' protested Pamela. 'Gloria just spoils him and it's natural.'

'I know he is, it's not his fault, but they will *force* him. Look at that snow-man—and staying behind to do it. A foul looking thing!'

'Perhaps his eyes played funny tricks with him,' said Pamela.

'What d'you mean by that?'

'I don't know why I said it,' said Pamela frowning, 'sort of echo, I suppose. Let's go to bed.'

Walter kissed her gently, but fervently, as he loved her. He was a one-lady's-man and had felt a bit nervous about her for a moment or two.

Was the house a little cooler? wondered Mr Braxton, as he was undressing, or was it that he was getting more used to it? He was now convinced that there was something wrong with the installation; he'd get an expert down. Meanwhile they must stick it. He yawned, wondered how Curtis was, and switched off the light.

Soon all the occupants were at rest and the great house swinging silently against the stars. Should have been at rest, rather, for one and all recalled that night with reluctance and dread. Their dreams were harsh and unhallowed, yet oddly related, being concerned with dim, uncertain and yet somehow urgent happenings in and around the house, as though some thing or things were stirring while they slept and communicated their motions to their dreaming consciousness. They awoke tired with a sense of unaccountable malaise.

Mrs Curtis rang up during breakfast and her voice revealed her distress. Timothy was delirious and much worse. The doctor was coming at 10.30.

Mr and Mrs Braxton decided to go over there, and sent for the car. Knowles was waiting just outside the house when they arrived.

'He's very bad,' he said quietly. 'I've sent for two nurses and Sir Arthur Galley; I want another opinion. Has he had some trouble with a tree?'

'Trouble with a tree!' said Mr Braxton his nerves giving a flick.

'Yes, it's probably just a haphazard, irrational idea of delirium, but he continually fusses about some tree.'

'How bad is he?' asked Mrs Braxton.

The doctor frowned. 'I wish I knew. I'm fairly out of my depth. He's keeping up his strength fairly well, but he can't go on like this.'

'As bad as that!' exclaimed Mr Braxton.

'I'm very much afraid so. I'm anxiously awaiting Sir Arthur's verdict. By the way, that cow-man is very ill indeed; I'm sending him into hospital.'

'What happened to him?' asked Mr Braxton, absently, his mind on Curtis.

'Apparently a branch of your Christmas tree snapped back at him and struck his face. Blood-poisoning set in almost at once.'

Mr Braxton felt that tremor again, but merely nodded.

'I was just wondering if there might be some connection between the two, that Curtis is blaming himself for the accident. Seems an absurd idea, but judging from his ravings he appears to think he is lashed to some tree and that the great heat he feels comes from it.'

They went into the house and did their best to comfort and reassure Mrs Curtis, instructed Knowles to ring up as soon as Sir Arthur's verdict was known, and then drove home.

The children had just come in from playing in the snow.

'Grandpa, the snow-man's melted,' said Paddy. 'Did it thaw in the night?'

'Must have done,' replied Mr Braxton, forcing a smile.

'Come and look, Grandpa,' persisted Paddy, 'there's nothing left of it.'

'Grandpa doesn't want to be bothered,' said Mary, noticing his troubled face.

'I'll come,' said Mr Braxton. When he reached the site of the snow-man his thoughts were still elsewhere, but his mind quickly re-focused itself, for he was faced with something a little strange. Not a vestige of the statue remained, though the snow was frozen crisp and crunched hard beneath their feet; and yet the snow-man was completely obliterated and where it had stood was a circle of bare, brown grass.

'It must have thawed in the night and then frozen again,' he said uncertainly.

'Then why—' began Paddy.

'Don't bother Grandpa,' said Mary sharply. 'He's told you what happened.'

They wandered off towards the heavy, hurrying river.

'Are those dog-paw marks?' asked Phyllis.

That reminded Mr Braxton. He peered down. 'Yes,' he replied. 'And I bet they're those of that brute of an Alsatian; it must be a colossal beast.'

'And it must have paws like a young bear,' laughed Mary. 'They're funny dogs, sort of Jekyll-and-Hydes. I rather adore them.'

'You wouldn't adore this devil. He's all Hyde.' (I'm in the wrong mood for these festivities, he thought irritably.)

During the afternoon George and Walter took the

kids to a cinema in Oxford; the others finished the decoration of the tree.

The presents, labelled with the names of their recipients, were arranged on tables round the room and the huge cracker, ten feet long and forty inches in circumference, was placed on its gaily decorated trestle near the tree. Just as the job was finished, Mary did a three-quarters faint, but was quickly revived with brandy.

'It's the simply ghastly heat in the house!' exclaimed Gloria, who was not looking too grand herself. 'The installation must be completely diseased. Ours always works perfectly.' Mary had her dinner in bed and Jack came up to her immediately he had finished his.

'How are you feeling, darling?' he asked.

'Oh, I'm all right.'

'It *was* the heat, of course?'

'Oh, yes,' replied Mary with rather forced emphasis.

'Scared you a bit, going off like that?' suggested Jack, regarding her rather sharply.

'I'm quite all right, thank you,' said Mary in the tone she always adopted when she'd had enough of a subject. 'I'd like to rest. Switch off the light.'

But when Jack had gone, she didn't close her eyes, but lay on her back staring up at the faint outline of the ceiling. She frowned and lightly chewed the little finger of her left hand, a habit of hers when unpleasantly puzzled. Mary, like most people of strong character and limited imagination, hated to be puzzled. Everything, she considered, ought to have a simple explanation if one tried hard enough to find it. But how could one explain this odd thing that had happened to her? Besides the grandiose gifts on the tables which bore a number, as well as the recipient's name, a small present for everyone was hung on the tree. This also bore a number, the same one as the lordly gift, so easing the Braxtons' task of handing these out to the right people.

Mary had just fixed Curtis's label to a cigarette lighter and tied it on the tree when it swung on its silk thread, so that the back of the card was visible; and on it was this inscription: 'Died, December 25th, 1938'. It spun away again and back and the inscription was no longer there.

Now Mary came of a family which rather prided itself on being unimaginative. Her father had confined his flights of fancy to the Annual Meeting of his shareholders, while, to her mother, imagination and mendacity were at least first cousins. So Mary could hardly credit the explanation that, being remotely worried about Mr Curtis, she had subconsciously concocted that sinister sentence. On the other hand she knew poor Mr Curtis was very ill and, therefore, perhaps if her brain had played that malign little trick on her, it might have done so in 'tombstone writing.'

This was a considerable logical exercise for Mary, the effort tired her, the impression began to fade and she started wondering how much longer Jack was going to sit up. She dozed off and there, as if flashed on the screen 'inside her head' was 'Died, December 25th, 1938'. This, oddly enough, completely reassured her. There was 'nothing there' this time. There had been nothing that other time. She'd been very weak and imaginative even to think otherwise.

While she was deciding this, Dr Knowles rang up. 'Sir Arthur has just been,' he said. 'And I'm sorry to say he's pessimistic. He says Curtis is very weak.'

'But what's the matter with him?' asked Mr Braxton urgently.

'He doesn't know. He calls it P.U.O. which really means nothing.'

'But what's it stand for?'

'Pyrexia unknown origin. There are some fevers which cannot be described more precisely.'

'How ill is he really?'

'All I can say is, we must hope for the best.'

'My God!' exclaimed Mr Braxton. 'When's Sir Arthur coming again?'

'At eleven tomorrow. I'll ring you up after he's been.'

Mr Braxton excused himself and went to his room. Like many men of his dominating, sometimes ruthless type, he was capable of an intensity of feeling, anger, resolution, desire for revenge, but also affection and sympathy, unknown to more superficially Christian and kindly souls. He was genuinely attached to Curtis and his wife and was very harshly and poignantly moved by this news which, he realised, could hardly have been worse. He would have to exercise all his willpower if he was to sleep.

If on the preceding night the rest of the sleepers had been broken by influences which had insinuated themselves into their dreams, that which caused the night of that Christmas Eve to be unforgettable was the demoniacal violence of the elements. The north-easter had been waxing steadily all the evening and by midnight reached hurricane force, driving before it an almost impenetrable wall of snow. Not only so, but continually all through the night the wall was enflamed, and the roar of the hurricane silenced, by fearful flashes of lightning and rafales of thunder. The combination was almost intolerably menacing. As the great house shook from the gale and trembled at the blasts and the windows blazed with strange polychromatic balls of flame, all were tense and troubled. The children fought or succumbed to their terror according to their natures; their parents soothed and reassured them.

Mr Braxton was convinced the lightning conductors were struck three times within five minutes, and he could imagine them recoiling from the mighty impacts and seething from the terrific charges. Not till a dilatory, chaotic dawn staggered up the sky did the storm temporarily lull. For a time the sky cleared and the frost came hard. It was a yawning and haggard company which assembled at breakfast. But determined efforts were made to engender a communal cheerfulness. Mr Braxton did his best to contribute his quota of seasonable bonhomie, but his mind was plagued by thoughts of Curtis. Before the meal was finished the vicar rang up to say the church tower had been struck and almost demolished, so there could be no services. It rang again to say that Brent's farmhouse had been burnt to the ground.

While the others went off to inspect the church, Mr Braxton remained in the study. Presently Knowles rang to say Sir Arthur had been and pronounced Curtis weaker, but his condition was not quite hopeless. One of the most ominous symptoms was the violence of the delirium. Curtis appeared to be in great terror and sedatives had no effect.

'How's that cow-man?' asked Mr Braxton.

'He died in the night, I'm sorry to say.'

Whereupon Mr Braxton broke one of his strictest rules by drinking a very stiff whisky with very little soda.

Christmas dinner was tolerably hilarious, and after it, the children, bulging and incipiently bilious, slept some of it off, while their elders put the final touches to the preparations for the party.

In spite of the weather, not a single 'cry-off' was telephoned. There was a good reason for this; Mr Braxton's entertainments were justly famous.

So from four-thirty onwards the 'Cream of North Berkshire Society' came ploughing through the snow to the Hall; Lady Pounser and party bringing up the rear in her heirloom Rolls which was dribbling steam from its ancient and aristocratic beak. A tea of teas, not merely a high-tea, an Everest tea, towering, sky-scraping, was then attacked by the already stuffed juveniles who, by the end of it, were almost livid with repletion, finding even the efforts of cracker-pulling almost beyond them.

They were then propelled into the library where rows of chairs had been provided for them. There was a screen at one end of the room, a projector at the other. Mr Braxton had provided one of his famous surprises! The room was darkened and on the screen was flashed the sentence: 'The North Berks News Reel'.

During the last few weeks Mr Braxton had had a sharp-witted and discreetly furtive camera-man at work shooting some of the guests while busy about their more or less lawful occasions.

For example, there was a sentence from a speech by Lord Gallen, the Socialist Peer: 'It is a damnable and calculated lie for our opponents to suggest we aim at a preposterous and essentially *inequitable* equalisation on income—' And then there was His Lordship just entering his limousine, and an obsequious footman, rug in hand, holding the door open for him.

His Lordship's laughter was raucous and vehement, though he *would* have liked to have said a few words in rebuttal.

And there was Lady Pounser's Rolls, locally known as 'the hippograffe' stuck in a snow-drift and enveloped in steam, with the caption, 'Oh, Mr Mercury, *do* give me a start!' And other kindly if slightly sardonic japes at the expense of the North Berks Cream.

The last scene was meant as an appropriate prelude to the climax of the festivities. It showed Curtis and his crew digging up the tree from Lucky Grove. Out they came from the holm oaks straining under their load, but close observers noticed there was one who remained behind, standing menacing and motionless, a very tall, dark, brooding figure. There came a blinding lightning flash which seemed to blaze sparking round the room, and a fearsome metallic bang. The storm had returned with rasping and imperious salute.

The lights immediately came on and the children were marshalled to the ballroom. As they entered and saw the high tree shining there and the little people so lively upon its branches a prolonged 'O—h!' of astonishment was exhorted from the blasé brats. But there was another wave of flame against the windows which rattled wildly at the ensuing roar, and the cries of delight were tinged with terror. And, indeed, the hard, blue glare flung a sinister glow on the tree and its whirling throng.

The grown-ups hastened to restore equanimity and, forming rings of children, circled the tree.

Presently Mrs Braxton exclaimed: 'Now then, look for your names on the cards and see what Father Christmas has brought you.'

Though hardly one of the disillusioned infants retained any belief in that superannuated Deliverer of Goods, the response was immediate. For they had sharp ears which had eagerly absorbed the tales of Braxton munificence. At the same time it was noticeable that some approached the tree with diffidence, almost reluctance, and started back as a livid flare broke against the window-blinds and the dread peals shook the streaming snow from the eaves.

Mary had just picked up little Angela Rayner so that she could reach her card, when the child screamed and pulled away her hand.

'The worm,' she cried, and a thick, black-grey squirming maggot fell from her fingers to the floor and writhed away. George, who was near, put his shoe on it with a squish.

One of the Pounser tribe, whose card was just below the Big Bad Wolf, refused to approach it. No wonder, thought Walter, for it looked horribly hunting and alive. There were other mischances too. The witch behind the sombre tree seemed to pounce out at Clarissa Balder, so she tearfully complained, and Gloria had to pull off her card for her. Of course Gregory was temperamental, seeming to stare at a spot just below the taut peak of the tree, as if mazed and entranced. But the presents were wonderful and more than worth the small ordeal of finding one's card and pretending not to be frightened when the whole room seemed full of fiery hands and the thunder cracked against one's ear-drums and shook one's teeth. Easy to be afraid!

At length the last present had been bestowed and it was time for the pièce de résistance, the pulling of the great cracker. Long, silken cords streamed from each end with room among them for fifty chubby fists, and a great surprise inside, for sure. The languid, uneasy troop were lined up at each end and took a grip on the silken cords.

At that moment a footman came in and told Mr Braxton he was wanted on the telephone.

Filled with foreboding he went to his study. He heard the voice of Knowles—

'I'm afraid I have very bad news for you . . .'

*

The chubby fists gripped the silken cords.

'Now pull!' cried Mrs Braxton.

The opposing teams took the strain.

A leaping flash and a blasting roar. The children were hurled, writhing and screaming over each other.

Up from the middle of the cracker leapt a rosy shaft of flame which, as it reached the ceiling, seemed to flatten its peak so that it resembled a great snake of fire which turned and hurled itself against the tree in a blinding embrace. There was a fierce sustained 'Hiss,' the tree flamed like a torch, and all the fairy globes upon it burst and splintered. And then the roaring torch cast itself down amongst the screaming chaos. For a moment the great pot, swathed in green, was a carmine cauldron and its paint streamed like blood upon the floor. Then the big room was a dream of fire and those within it driven wildly from its heat.

*

Phil Tangler, whose farmhouse, on the early slopes of Missen Rise, overlooked both Lucky's Grove and the Hall, solemnly declared that at 7.30 on Christmas Day, 1938, he was watching from a window and marvelling at the dense and boiling race of snow, the bitter gale, and the wicked flame and fury of the storm, when he saw a huge fist of fire form a rift in the cloud-rack, a fist with two huge blazing fingers, one of which speared down on the Hall, another touched and kindled the towering fir in Lucky's Grove, as though saluting it. Five minutes later he was racing through the hurricane to join in a vain night-long fight to save the Hall, already blazing from stem to stern.

The Moon Bog

H. P. LOVECRAFT

Somewhere, to what remote and fearsome region I know not, Denys Barry has gone. I was with him the last night he lived among men, and heard his screams when the thing came to him; but all the peasants and police in County Meath could never find him, or the others, though they searched long and far. And now I shudder when I hear the frogs piping in swamps, or see the moon in lonely places.

I had known Denys Barry well in America, where he had grown rich, and had congratulated him when he bought back the old castle by the bog at sleepy Kilderry. It was from Kilderry that his father had come, and it was there that he wished to enjoy his wealth among ancestral scenes. Men of his blood had once ruled over Kilderry and built and dwelt in the castle, but those days were very remote, so that for generations the castle had been empty and decaying. After he went to Ireland Barry wrote to me often, and told me how under his care the grey castle was rising tower by tower to its ancient splendour, how the ivy was climbing slowly over the restored walls as it had climbed so many centuries ago, and how the peasants blessed him for bringing back the old days with his gold from over the sea. But in time there came troubles, and the peasants ceased to bless him, and fled away instead as from a doom. And then he sent a letter and asked me to visit him, for he was lonely in the castle with no one to speak to save the new servants and labourers he had brought from the North.

The bog was the cause of all these troubles, as Barry told me the night I came to the castle. I had reached

Kilderry in the summer sunset, as the gold of the sky lighted the green of the hills and groves and the blue of the bog, where on a far islet a strange olden ruin glistened spectrally. The sunset was very beautiful, but the peasants at Ballylough had warned me against it and said that Kilderry had become accursed, so that I almost shuddered to see the high turrets of the castle gilded with fire. Barry's motor had met me at the Ballylough station, for Kilderry is off the railway. The villagers had shunned the car and the driver from the North, but had whispered to me with pale faces when they saw I was going to Kilderry. And that night, after our reunion, Barry told me why.

The peasants had gone from Kilderrry because Denys Barry was to drain the great bog. For all his love of Ireland, America had not left him untouched, and he hated the beautiful wasted space where peat might be cut and land opened up. The legends and superstitions of Kilderry did not move him, and he laughed when the peasants first refused to help, and then cursed him and went away to Ballylough with their few belongings as they saw his determination. In their place he sent for labourers from the North, and when the servants left he replaced them likewise. But it was lonely among strangers, so Barry had asked me to come.

When I heard the fears which had driven the people from Kilderry I laughed as loudly as my friend had laughed, for these fears were of the vaguest, wildest, and most absurd character. They had to do with some preposterous legend of the bog, and of a grim guardian spirit that dwelt in the strange olden ruin on the far islet I had seen in the sunset. There were tales of dancing lights in the dark of the moon, and of chill winds when the night was warm; of wraiths in white hovering over the waters, and of an imagined city of stone deep down below the swampy surface. But hovering over the waters, and of an imagined absolute unanimity, was that of the curse awaiting him who should dare to touch or drain the vast reddish morass. There were secrets, said the peasants, which must not be uncovered; secrets that had lain hidden since the plague came to the children of Partholan in the fabulous years beyond history. In the *Book of Invaders* it is told that these sons of the Greeks were all buried at Tallaght, but old men in Kilderry said that one city was overlooked save by its patron moon-goddess; so that only the wooded hills buried it when the men of Nemed swept down from Scythia in their thirty ships.

Such were the idle tales which had made the villagers leave Kilderry, and when I heard them I did not wonder that Denys Barry had refused to listen. He had, however, a great interest in antiquities, and proposed to explore the bog thoroughly when it was drained. The white ruins on the islet he had often visited, but though their age was plainly great, and their contour very little like that of most ruins in Ireland, they were too dilapidated to tell the days of their glory. Now the work of drainage was ready to begin, and the labourers from the North were soon to strip the forbidden bog of its green moss and red heather, and kill the tiny shell-paved streamlets and quiet blue pools fringed with rushes.

After Barry had told me these things I was very drowsy, for the travels of the day had been wearying and my host had talked late into the night. A manservant showed me to my room, which was in a remote tower overlooking the village, and the plain at the edge of the bog, and the bog itself; so that I could see from my windows in the moonlight the silent roofs from which the peasants had fled and which now sheltered the labourers from the North, and too, the parish church with its antique spire. and far out across the brooding bog the remote olden ruin on the islet gleaming white and spectral. Just as I dropped to sleep I fancied I heard faint sounds from the distance; sounds that were wild and half musical, and stirred me with a weird excitement which coloured my dreams. But when I awakened next morning I felt it had all been a dream, for the visions I had seen were more wonderful than any sounds of wild pipes in the night. Influenced by the legends that Barry had related, my mind had in slumber hovered around a stately city in a green valley, where marble streets and statues, villas and temples, carvings and inscriptions, all spoke in certain tones the glory that was Greece. When I told this dream to Barry we both laughed; but I laughed the louder, because he was perplexed about his labourers from the North. For the sixth time they had all overslept, waking very slowly and dazedly, and acting as if they had not rested, although they were known to have gone early to bed the night before.

That morning and afternoon I wandered alone through the sun-gilded village and talked now and then with idle labourers, for Barry was busy with the final plans for beginning his work of drainage. The labourers were not as happy as they might have been, for most of them seemed uneasy over some dream which they had had, yet which they tried in vain to remember. I told them of my dream, but they were not interested till I spoke of the weird sounds I thought I had heard. Then they looked oddly at me, and said that they seemed to remember weird sounds, too.

In the evening Barry dined with me and announced that he would begin the drainage in two days. I was glad, for although I disliked to see the moss and the heather and the little streams and lakes depart, I had a growing wish to discern the ancient secrets the deep-matted peat might hide. And that night my dreams of piping flutes and marble peristyle came to a sudden and disquieting end; for upon the city in the valley

I saw a pestilence descend, and then a frightful avalanche of wooded slopes that covered the dead bodies in the streets and left unburied only the temples of Artemis on the high peak, where the aged moon-priestess Cleis lay cold and silent with a crown of ivory on her silver head.

I have said that I awakened suddenly and in alarm. For some time I could not tell whether I was waking or sleeping, for the sound of flutes still rang shrilly in my ears; but when I saw on the floor the icy moon-beams and the outlines of a latticed Gothic window I decided I must be awake and in the castle of Kilderry. Then I heard a clock from some remote landing below strike the hour of two, and knew I was awake. Yet still there came that monotonous piping from afar; wild, weird airs that made me think of some dance of fauns on distant Maenalus. It would not let me sleep, and in impatience I sprang up and paced the floor. Only by chance did I go to the north window and look out upon the silent village and the plain at the edge of the bog. I had no wish to gaze abroad, for I wanted to sleep; but the flutes tormented me, and I had to do or see something. How could I have suspected the thing I was to behold?

There in the moonlight that flooded the spacious plain was a spectacle which no mortal, having seen it, could ever forget. To the sound of reedy pipes that echoed over the bog there glided silently and eerily a mixed throng of swaying figures, reeling through such a revel as the Sicilians may have danced to Demeter in the old days under the harvest moon beside the Cyane. The wide plain, the golden moonlight, the shadowy moving forms, and above all the shrill monotonous piping, produced an effect which almost paralysed me; yet I noted amidst my fear that half of these tireless, mechanical dancers were the labourers whom I had thought asleep, whilst the other half were strange airy beings in white, half-indeterminate in nature, but suggesting pale wistful naiads from the haunted fountains of the bog. I do not know how long I gazed at this sight from the lonely turret window before I dropped suddenly in a dreamless swoon, out of which the high sun of morning aroused me.

My first impulse on awaking was to communicate all my fears and observations to Denys Barry, but as I saw the sunlight glowing through the latticed east window I became sure that there was no reality in what I thought I had seen. I am given to strange fantasms, yet am never weak enough to believe in them; so on this occasion contented myself with questioning the labourers, who slept very late and recalled nothing of the previous night save misty dreams of shrill sounds. This matter of the spectral piping harassed me greatly, and I wondered if the crickets of autumn had come before their time to vex the night and haunt the visions of men. Later in the day I watched Barry in the library poring over his plans for the great work which was to begin on the morrow, and for the first time felt a touch of the same kind of fear that had driven the peasants away. For some unknown reason I dreaded the thought of disturbing the ancient bog and its sunless secrets, and pictured terrible sights lying black under the unmeasured depth of age-old peat. That these secrets should be brought to light seemed injudicious, and I began to wish for an excuse to leave the castle and the village. I went so far as to talk casually to Barry on the subject, but did not dare continue after he gave his resounding laugh. So I was silent when the sun set fulgently over the far hills, and Kilderry blazed all red and gold in a flame that seemed a portent.

Whether the events of that night were reality or illusion I shall never ascertain. Certainly they transcend anything we dream of in nature and the universe;

yet in no normal fashion can I explain those disappearances which were known to all men after it was over. I retired early and full of dread, and for a long time could not sleep in the uncanny silence of the tower. It was very dark, for although the sky was clear the moon was now well on the wane, and would not rise till the small hours. I thought as I lay there of Denys Barry, and of what would befall that bog when the day came, and found myself almost frantic with an impulse to rush out into the night, take Barry's car, and drive madly to Ballylough out of the menaced lands. But before my fears could crystallise into action I had fallen asleep, and gazed in dreams upon the city in the valley, cold and dead under a shroud of hideous shadow.

Probably it was the shrill piping that awaked me, yet that piping was not what I noticed first when I opened my eyes. I was lying with my back to the east window overlooking the bog, where the waning moon would rise, and therefore expected to see light cast on the opposite wall before me; but I had not looked for such a sight as now appeared. Light indeed glowed on the panels ahead, but it was not any light that the moon gives. Terrible and piercing was the shaft of ruddy refulgence that streamed through the Gothic window, and the whole chamber was brilliant with a splendour intense and unearthly. My immediate actions were peculiar for such a situation, but it is only in tales that a man does the dramatic and foreseen thing. Instead of looking out across the bog, toward the source of the new light, I kept my eyes from the window in panic fear, and clumsily drew on my clothing with some dazed idea of escape. I remember seizing my revolver and hat, but before it was over I had lost them both without firing the one or donning the other. After a time the fascination of the red radiance overcame my fright, and I crept to the east window and looked out whilst the maddening, incessant piping whined and reverberated through the castle and over all the village.

Over the bog was a deluge of flaring light, scarlet and sinister, and pouring from the strange olden ruin on the far islet. The aspect of that ruin I cannot describe—I must have been mad, for it seemed to rise majestic and undecayed, splendid and column-cinctured, the flame-reflecting marble of its entablature piercing the sky like the apex of a temple on a mountain-top. Flutes shrieked and drums began to beat, and as I watched in awe and terror I thought I saw dark saltant forms silhouetted grotesquely against the vision of marble and effulgence. The effect was titanic—altogether unthinkable—and I might have stared indefinitely had not the sound of the piping seemed to grow stronger at my left. Trembling with a terror oddly mixed with ecstasy I crossed the circular room to the north window from which I could see the village and the plain at the edge of the bog. There my eyes dilated again with a wild wonder as great as if I had not just turned from a scene beyond the pale of nature, for on the ghastly red-lit plain was moving a procession of beings in such a manner as none ever saw before save in nightmares.

Half gliding, half floating in the air, the white-clad bog-wraiths were slowly retreating toward the still waters and the island ruin in fantastic formations suggesting some ancient and solemn ceremonial dance. Their waving translucent arms, guided by the detestable piping of those unseen flutes, beckoned in uncanny rhythm to a throng of lurching labourers who followed doglike with blind, brainless, floundering steps as if dragged by a clumsy but resistless demon-will. As the naiads neared the bog, without altering their course, a new line of stumbling stragglers zigzagged drunkenly out of the castle from some door far below my window, groped sightlessly across the courtyard and through the intervening bit of village, and joined the floundering column of labourers on the plain. Despite their distance below me I at once knew they were the servants brought from the North, for I recognised the ugly and unwieldy form of the cook, whose very absurdness had now become unutterably tragic. The flutes piped horribly, and again I heard the beating of the drums from the direction of the island ruin. Then silently and gracefully the naiads reached the water and melted one by one into the ancient bog; while the line of followers, never checking their speed, splashed awkwardly after them and vanished amidst a tiny vortex of unwholesome bubbles which I could barely see in the scarlet light. And as the last pathetic straggler, the fat cook, sank heavily out of sight in that sullen pool, the flutes and the drums grew silent, and the blinding red rays from the ruins snapped instantaneously out, leaving the village of doom lone and desolate in the wan beams of a new-risen moon.

My condition was now one of indescribable chaos. Not knowing whether I was mad or sane, sleeping or waking, I was saved only by a merciful numbness. I believe I did ridiculous things such as offering prayers to Artemis, Latona, Demeter, Persephone and Plouton. All that I recalled of a classical youth came to my lips as the horrors of the situation roused my deepest superstitions. I felt that I had witnessed the death of a whole village, and knew I was alone in the castle with Denys Barry, whose boldness had brought down a doom. As I thought of him new terrors convulsed me, and I fell to the floor, not fainting, but physically helpless. Then I felt the icy blast from the east window where the moon had risen, and began to hear the shrieks in the castle far below me. Soon these shrieks had attained a magnitude and quality which cannot be written of, and which make me faint as I think of them. All I can say is that they came from

somcthing I had known as a friend.

At some time during this shocking period the cold wind and the screaming must have roused me, for my next impression is of racing madly through inky rooms and corridors and out across the courtyard into the hideous night. They found me at dawn wandering mindless near Ballylough, but what unhinged me utterly was not any of the horrors I had seen or heard before. What I muttered about as I came slowly out of the shadows was a pair of fantastic incidents which occurred in my flight: incidents of no significance, yet which haunt me unceasingly when I am alone in certain marshy places or in the moonlight.

As I fled from that accursed castle along the bog's edge I heard a new sound: common, yet unlike any I had heard before at Kilderry. The stagnant waters, lately quite devoid of animal life, now teemed with a horde of slimy enormous frogs which piped shrilly and incessantly in tones strangely out of keeping with their size. They glistened bloated and green in the moonbeams, and seemed to gaze up at the fount of light. I followed the gaze of one very fat and ugly frog, and saw the second of the things which drove my senses away.

Stretching directly from the strange olden ruin on the far islet to the waning moon, my eyes seemed to trace a beam of faint quivering radiance having no reflection in the waters of the bog. And upward along that pallid path my fevered fancy pictured a thin shadow slowly writhing, a vague contorted shadow struggling as if drawn by unseen demons. Crazed as I was, I saw in that awful shadow a monstrous resemblance—a nauseous, unbelievable caricature—a blasphemous effigy of him who had been Denys Barry.

The White Cat of Drumgunniol

J. S. LEFANU

There is a famous story of a white cat, with which we all become acquainted in the nursery. I am going to tell a story of a white cat very different from the amiable and enchanted princess who took that disguise for a season. The white cat of which I speak was a more sinister animal.

The traveller from Limerick towards Dublin, after

passing the hills of Killaloe upon the left, as Keeper Mountain raises high in view, finds himself gradually hemmed in, up the right, by a range of lower hills. An undulating plain that dips gradually to a lower level than that of the road interposes, and some scattered hedgerows relieve its somewhat wild and melancholy character.

One of the few human habitations that send up their films of turf-smoke from that lonely plain, is the loosely-thatched, earth-built dwelling of a 'strong farmer', as the more prosperous of the tenant-farming classes are termed in Munster. It stands in a clump of trees near the edge of a wandering stream, about half-way between the mountains and the Dublin road, and had been for generations tenanted by people named Donovan.

In a distant place, desirous of studying some Irish records which had fallen into my hands, and inquiring for a teacher capable of instructing me in the Irish language, a Mr Donovan, dreamy, harmless and learned, was recommended to me for the purpose.

I found that he had been educated as a Sizar in Trinity College, Dublin. He now supported himself by teaching, and the special direction of my studies, I suppose, flattered his national partialities, for he unbosomed himself of much of his long-reserved thoughts, and recollections about his country and his early days. It was he who told me this story, and I mean to repeat it, as nearly as I can, in his own words.

I have myself seen the old farm-house, with its orchard of huge mossgrown apple trees. I have looked round on the peculiar landscape; the roofless, ivied tower, that two hundred years before had afforded a refuge from raid and rapparee, and which still occupies its old place in the angle of the haggard; the bush-grown 'liss', that scarcely a hundred and fifty steps away records the labours of a bygone race; the dark and towering outline of old Keeper in the background;

and the lonely range of furze and heath-clad hills that form a nearer barrier, with many a line of grey rock and clump of dwarf oak or birch. The pervading sense of loneliness made it a scene not unsuited for a wild and unearthly story. And I could quite fancy how, seen in the grey of a wintry morning, shrouded far and wide in snow, or in the melancholy glory of an autumnal sunset, or in the chill splendour of a moonlight night, it might have helped to tone a dreamy mind like honest Dan Donovan's to superstition and a proneness to the illusions of fancy. It is certain, however, that I never anywhere met with a more simple-minded creature, or one on whose good faith I could more entirely rely.

When I was a boy, said he, living at home at Drumgunniol, I used to take my Goldsmith's *Roman History* in my hand and go down to my favourite seat, the flat stone, sheltered by a hawthorn tree beside the little lough, a large and deep pool, such as I have heard called a tarn in England. It lay in the gentle hollow of a field that is overhung toward the north by the old orchard, and being a deserted place was favourable to my studious quietude.

One day reading here, as usual, I wearied at last, and began to look about me, thinking of the heroic scenes I had just been reading of. I was as wide awake as I am at this moment, and I saw a woman appear at the corner of the orchard and walk down the slope. She wore a long, light grey dress, so long that it seemed to sweep the grass behind her, and so singular was her appearance in a part of the world where female attire is so inflexibly fixed by custom, that I could not take my eyes off her. Her course lay diagonally from corner to corner of the field, which was a large one, and she pursued it without swerving.

When she came near I could see that her feet were bare, and that she seemed to be looking steadfastly upon some remote object for guidance. Her route would have crossed me—had the tarn not interposed—about ten or twelve yards below the point at which I was sitting. But instead of arresting her course at the margin of the lough, as I had expected, she went on without seeming conscious of its existence, and I saw her, as plainly as I see you, sir, walk across the surface of the water, and pass, without seeming to see me, at about the distance I had calculated.

I was ready to faint from sheer terror. I was only thirteen years old then, and I remember every particular as if it had happened this hour.

The figure passed through the gap at the far corner of the field, and there I lost sight of it. I had hardly strength to walk home, and was so nervous, and ultimately so ill, that for three weeks I was confined to the house, and could not bear to be alone for a moment. I never entered that field again, such was the horror with which from that moment every object in it was clothed. Even at this distance of time I should not like to pass through it.

This apparition I connected with a mysterious event; and, also, with a singular liability, that has for nearly eighty years distinguished, or rather afflicted, our family. It is no fancy. Everybody in that part of the country knows all about it. Everybody connected what I had seen with it.

I will tell it all to you as well as I can.

When I was about fourteen years old—that is about a year after the sight I had seen in the lough field—we were one night expecting my father home from the fair of Killaloe. My mother sat up to welcome him home and I with her, for I liked nothing better than such a vigil. My brothers and sisters, and the farm servants, except the men who were driving home the cattle from the fair, were asleep in their beds. My mother and I were sitting in the chimney corner chatting together, and watching my father's supper, which was kept hot over the fire. We knew that he would return before the men who were driving home the cattle, for he was riding, and told us that he would only wait to see them fairly on the road, and then push homeward.

At length we heard his voice and the knocking of his loaded whip at the door, and my mother let him in. I don't think I ever saw my father drunk, which is more than most men of my age, from the same part of the country, could say of theirs. But he could drink his glass of whisky as well as another, and he usually came home from fair or market a little merry and mellow, and with a jolly flush in his cheeks.

Tonight he looked sunken, pale and sad. He entered with the saddle and bridle in his hand, and he dropped them against the wall, near the door, and put his arms round his wife's neck, and kissed her kindly.

'Welcome home, Meehal,' said she, kissing him heartily.

'God bless you, mavourneen,' he answered.

And hugging her again, he turned to me, who was plucking him by the hand, jealous of his notice. I was little, and light of my age, and he lifted me up in his arms and kissed me, and my arms being about his neck, he said to my mother:

'Draw the bolt, acuishla.'

She did so, and setting me down very dejectedly, he walked to the fire and sat down on a stool, and stretched his feet toward the glowing turf, leaning with his hands on his knees.

'Rouse up, Mick, darlin',' said my mother, who was growing anxious, 'and tell me how did the cattle sell, and did everything go lucky at the fair, or is there anything wrong with the landlord, or what in the world is it that ails you, Mick, jewel?'

'Nothin', Molly. The cows sould well, thank God, and there's nothin' fell out between me an' the landlord, an' everything's the same way. There's no fault to find anywhere.'

'Well, then, Mickey, since so it is, turn round to your hot supper, and ate it, and tell us is there anything new.'

'I got my supper, Molly, on the way, and I can't ate a bit,' he answered.

'Got your supper on the way, an' you knowin' 'twas waiting for you at home, an' your wife sitting up an' all!' cried my mother reproachfully.

'You're takin' a wrong meanin' out of what I say,' said my father. 'There's something happened that leaves me that I can't ate a mouthful, and I'll not be dark with you, Molly, for, maybe it ain't very long I have to be here an' I'll tell you what it was. It's what I've seen, the white cat.'

'The Lord between us and harm!' exclaimed my mother, in a moment as pale and as chap-fallen as my father; and then, trying to rally, with a laugh, she said: 'Ha! 'tis only funnin' me you are. Sure a white rabbit was snared a Sunday last, in Grady's wood; an Teigue seen a big white rat in the haggard yesterday.'

''Twas neither rat nor rabbit was in it. Don't ye think but I'd know a rat or a rabbit from a big white cat, with green eyes as big as halfpennies, and its back riz up like a bridge, trottin' on and across me, and ready, if I dar' stop, to rub its sides against my shins, and maybe to make a jump and seize my throat, if that it's a cat, at all, an' not something worse?'

As he ended his description in a low tone, looking straight at the fire, my father drew his big hand across his forehead once or twice, his face being damp and shining with the moisture of fear, and he sighed, or rather groaned, heavily.

My mother had relapsed into panic, and was praying again in her fear. I, too, was terribly frightened, and on the point of crying, for I knew all about the white cat.

Clapping my father on the shoulder, by way of encouragement, my mother leaned over him, kissing him, and at last began to cry. He was wringing her hands in his, and seemed in great trouble.

'There was nothin' came into the house with me?' he asked, in a very low tone, turning to me.

'There was nothin', father,' I said, 'but the saddle and bridle that was in your hand.'

'Nothin' white kem in at the doore wid me?' he repeated.

'Nothin' at all,' I answered.

'So be it,' said my father, and making the sign of the cross, he began mumbling to himself, and I knew he was saying his prayers.

Waiting for a while, to give him time for this exercise, my mother asked him where he first saw it.

'When I was riding up the bohereen,'—the Irish term meaning a little road, such as leads up to a farmhouse—'I bethought myself that the men was on the road with the cattle, and no one to look to the horse barrin' myself, so I thought I might as well leave him in the crooked field below, an' I tuck him there, he bein' cool, and not a hair turned, for I rode him aisy all the way. It was when I turned, after lettin' him go—the saddle and bridle bein' in my hand—that I saw it, pushin' out o' the long grass at the side o' the path, an' it walked across it, in front of me, an' then back again, before me, the same way, an' sometimes at one side, an' then at the other, lookin' at me wid them shinin' eyes; and I consayted I heard it growlin' as it kep' beside me—as close as ever you see—till I kem up to the doore, here, an' knocked an' called, as ye heerd me.'

Now, what was it, in so simple an incident, that agitated my father, my mother, myself, and finally, every member of this rustic household, with a terrible foreboding? It was this that we, one and all, believed that my father had received, in thus encountering the white cat, a warning of his approaching death.

The omen had never failed hitherto. It did not fail now. In a week my father took the fever that was going, and before a month he was dead.

My honest friend, Dan Donovan, paused here; I could perceive that he was praying, for his lips were busy, and I concluded that it was for the repose of that departed soul.

In a little while he resumed.

It is eighty years now since that omen first attached to my family. Eighty years? Aye, is it? Ninety is nearer the mark. And I have spoken to many old people, in those earlier times, who had a distinct recollection of everything connected with it.

It happened in this way.

My grand-uncle, Connor Donovan, had the old farm of Drumgunniol in his day. He was richer than ever my father was, or my father's father either, for he took a short lease of Balraghan, and made money of it. But money won't soften a hard heart, and I'm afraid my grand-uncle was a cruel man—a profligate man he was, surely, and that is mostly a cruel man at heart. He drank his share, too, and cursed and swore, when he was vexed, more than was good for his soul, I'm afraid.

At that time there was a beautiful girl of the Colemans, up in the mountains, not far from Capper Cullen. I'm told that there are no Colemans there now at all, and that family has passed away. The famine years made great changes.

Ellen Coleman was her name. The Colemans were not rich. But, being such a beauty, she might have made a good match. Worse than she did for herself, poor thing, she could not.

Con Donovan—my grand-uncle, God forgive him!—sometimes in his rambles saw her at fairs or patterns, and he fell in love with her, as who might not?

He used her ill. He promised her marriage, and persuaded her to come away with him; and, after all, he broke his word. It was just the old story. He tired of her, and he wanted to push himself in the world; and he married a girl of the Collopys, that had a great fortune—twenty-four cows, seventy sheep, and a hundred and twenty goats.

He married this Mary Callopy, and grew richer than before; and Ellen Coleman died broken-hearted. But that did not trouble the strong farmer much.

He would have liked to have children, but he had none, and this was the only cross he had to bear, for everything else went much as he wished.

One night he was returning from the fair of Nenagh. A shallow stream at that time crossed the road—they have thrown a bridge over it, I am told, some time since—and its channel was often dry in summer weather. When it was so, as it passes close by the old farm-house of Drumgunniol, without a great deal of winding, it makes a sort of road, which people then used as a short cut to reach the house by. Into this dry channel, as there was plenty of light from the moon, my grand-uncle turned his horse, and when he reached the two ash-trees at the meeting of the farm he turned his horse short into the river-field, intending to ride through the gap at the other end, under the oak-trees, and so he would have been within a few hundred yards of his door.

As he approached the 'gap' he saw, or thought he saw, with a slow motion, gliding along the ground towards the same point, and now and then with a soft bound, a white object, which he described as being no bigger than his hat, but what it was he could not see, as it moved along the hedge and disappeared at the point to which he himself was tending.

When he reached the gap the horse stopped short. He

urged and coaxed it in vain. He got down to lead it through, but it recoiled, snorted and fell into a wild trembling fit. He mounted it again. But its terror continued, and it obstinately resisted his caresses and his whip. It was bright moonlight, and my grand-uncle was chafed by the horse's resistance, and, seeing nothing to account for it, and being so near home, what little patience he possessed forsook him, and, plying his whip and spur in earnest, he broke into oaths, and curses.

All of a sudden the horse sprang through, and Con Donovan, as he passed under the broad branch of the oak, saw clearly a woman standing on the bank beside him, her arm extended, with the hand of which, as he flew by, she struck him a blow upon the shoulders. It threw him forward upon the neck of the horse, which, in wild terror, reached the door at a gallop, and stood there quivering and steaming all over.

Less alive than dead, my grand-uncle got in. He told his story, at least, so much as he chose. His wife did not quite know what to think. But that something very bad had happened she could not doubt. He was very faint and ill, and begged the priest should be sent for forthwith. When they were getting him to his bed they saw distinctly the marks of five fingerpints on the flesh of his shoulder, where the spectral blow had fallen. These singular marks—which they said resembled in tint the hue of a body struck by lightning—remained imprinted on his flesh, and were buried with him.

When he had recovered sufficiently to talk with the people about him—speaking, like a man at his last hour, from a burdened heart, and troubled conscience—he repeated his story, but said he did not see, or, at all events, know, the face of the figure that stood in the gap. No one believed him. He told more about it to the priest than to others. He certainly had a secret to tell. He might as well have divulged it frankly, for the neighbours all knew well enough that it was the face of dead Ellen Coleman that he had seen.

From that moment my grand-uncle never raised his head. He was a scared, silent, broken-spirited man. It was early summer then, and at the fall of the leaf in the same year he died.

Of course there was a wake, such as beseemed a strong farmer so rich as he. For some reason the arrangements of this ceremonial were a little different from the usual routine.

The usual practice is to place the body in the great room, or kitchen, as it is called, of the house. In this particular case there was, as I told you, for some reason, an unusual arrangement. The body was placed in a small room that opened upon the greater one. The door of this, during the wake, stood open. There were candles about the bed, and pipes and tobacco on the table, and stools for such guests as chose to enter, the door standing open for their reception.

The body, having been laid out, was left alone, in this smaller room, during the preparation for the wake. After nightfall one of the women, approaching the bed to get a chair which she had left near it, rushed from the room with a scream, and, having recovered her speech at the further end of the 'kitchen', and surrounded by a gaping audience, she said, at last:

'May I never sin, if his face bain't riz up again the back o' the bed, and he starin' down to the doore, wid eyes as big as pewter plates, that id be shinin' in the moon!'

'Arra, woman! Is it cracked you are?' said one of the farm boys as they are termed being men of any age you please.

'Agh, Molly, don't be talkin', woman! 'Tis what ye consayted it, goin' into the dark room, out o' the light. Why didn't ye take a candle in your fingers, ye aumadhaun?' said one of her female companions.

'Candle, or no candle, I seen it,' insisted Molly. 'An' what's more, I could a'most tak' my oath I seen his arum, too, stretchin' out o' the bed along the flure, three times as long as it should be, to take hould o' me be the fut.'

'Nansinse, ye fool, what id he want o' yer fut?' exclaimed one scornfully.

'Gi' me the candle, some o' yez—in the name o' God,' said old Sal Doolan, that was straight and lean, and a woman that could pray like a priest almost.

'Give her a candle,' agreed all.

But whatever they might say, there wasn't one among them that did not look pale and stern enough as they followed Mrs Doolan, who was praying as fast as her lips could patter, and leading the van with a tallow candle, held like a taper, in her fingers.

The door was half open, as the panic-stricken girl had left it; and holding the candle on high the better to examine the room, she made a step or so into it.

If my grand-uncle's hand had been stretched along the floor, in the unnatural way described, he had drawn it back again under the sheet that covered him. And tall Mrs Doolan was in no danger of tripping over his arm as she entered. But she had not gone more than a step or two with her candle aloft, when, with a drowning face, she suddenly stopped short, staring at the bed which was now fully in view.

'Lord, bless us, Mrs Doolan, ma'am, come back,' said the woman next her, who had fast hold of her dress, or her 'coat' as they call it, and drawing her backwards with a frightened pluck, while a general recoil among her followers betokened the alarm which her hesitation had inspired.

'Whisht, will yez?' said the leader, peremptorily, 'I can't hear my own ears wid the noise ye're making, an' which iv yez let the cat in here, an' whose cat is it?'

she asked peering suspiciously at a white cat that was sitting on the breast of the corpse.

'Put it away, will yez?' she resumed, with horror at the profanation. 'Many a corpse as I sthretched and crossed in the bed the likes o' that I never seen yet. The man o' the house, wid a brute baste like that mounted on him, like a phooka, Lord forgi' me for namin' the like in this room. Dhrive it away, some o' yez! Out o' that, this minute, I tell ye.'

Each repeated the order, but no one seemed inclined to execute it. They were crossing themselves, and whispering their conjectures and misgivings as to the nature of the beast, which was no cat of that house, nor one that they had ever seen before. On a sudden, the white cat placed itself on the pillow over the head of the body, and having from that place glared for a time at them over the features of the corpse, it crept softly along the body towards them, growling low and fiercely as it drew near.

Out of the room they bounced, in dreadful confusion, shutting the door fast after them, and not for a good while did the hardiest venture to peep in again.

The white cat was sitting in its old place, on the dead man's breast, but this time it crept quietly down the side of the bed, and disappeared under it, the sheet which was spread like a coverlet, and hung down nearly to the floor, concealing it from view.

Praying, crossing themselves, and not forgetting a sprinkling of holy water, they peeped, and finally searched, poking spades, 'wattles', pitchforks and such implements under the bed. But the cat was not to be found, and they concluded that it had made its escape among their feet as they stood near the threshold. So they secured the door carefully, with hasp and padlock.

But when the door was opened next morning they found the white cat sitting, as if it had never been disturbed, upon the breast of the dead man.

Again occurred very nearly the same scene with a like result, only that some said they saw the cat afterwards lurking under a big box in a corner of the outer-room, where my grand-uncle kept his leases and papers, and his prayer-book and beads.

Mrs Doolan heard it growling at her heels wherever she went; and although she could not see it, she could hear it spring on the back of her chair when she sat down, and growl in her ear, so that she would bounce up with a scream and a prayer, fancying that it was on the point of taking her by the throat.

And the priest's boy, looking round the corner, under the branches of the old orchard, saw a white cat sitting under the little window of the room where my grand-uncle was laid out and looking up at the four small panes of glass as a cat will watch a bird.

The end of it was that the cat was found on the corpse again, when the room was visited, and do what they might, whenever the body was left alone, the cat was found again in the same ill-omened contiguity with the dead man. And this continued, to the scandal and fear of the neighbourhood, until the door was opened finally for the wake.

My grand-uncle being dead, and, with all due solemnities, buried, I have done with him. But not quite yet with the white cat. No banshee ever yet was more inalienably attached to a family than this ominous apparition is to mine. But there is this difference. The banshee seems to be animated with an affectionate sympathy with the bereaved family to whom it is hereditarily attached, whereas this thing has about it a suspicion of malice. It is the messenger simply of death. And its taking the shape of a cat—the coldest, and they say, the most vindictive of brutes—is indicative of the spirit of its visit.

When my grandfather's death was near, although he

seemed quite well at the time, it appeared not exactly, but very nearly in the same way in which I told you it showed itself to my father.

The day before my Uncle Teigue was killed by the bursting of his gun, it appeared to him in the evening, at twilight, by the lough, in the field where I saw the woman who walked across the water, as I told you. My uncle was washing the barrel of his gun in the lough. The grass is short there, and there is no cover near it. He did not know how it approached but the first he saw of it, the white cat was walking close round his feet, in the twilight, with an angry twist of its tail, and a green glare in its eyes, and do what he would, it continued walking round and round him, in larger or smaller circles, till he reached the orchard, and there he lost it.

My poor Aunt Peg—she married one of the O'Brians, near Oolah—came to Drumgunniol to go to the funeral of a cousin who died about a mile away. She died herself, poor woman, only a month after.

Coming from the wake, at two or three o'clock in the morning, as she got over the stile into the farm of Drumgunniol, she saw the white cat at her side, and it kept close beside her, she ready to faint all the time, till she reached the door of the house, where it made a spring up into the white-thorn tree that grows close by, and so it parted from her. And my little brother Jim saw it also, just three weeks before he died. Every member of our family who dies, or takes his death-sickness at Drumgunniol, is sure to see the white cat, and no one of us who sees it need hope for long life after.

The Bottle Imp

R. L. STEVENSON

There was a man of the island of Hawaii, whom I shall call Kcawe; for the truth is, he still lives, and his name must be kept secret; but the place of his birth was not far from Honaunau, where the bones of Keawe the Great lie hidden in a cave. This man was poor, brave, and active; he could read and write like a schoolmaster; he was a first-rate mariner besides, sailed for some time in the island steamers, and steered a whale-boat on the Hamakua coast. At length it came in Keawe's mind to have a sight of the great world and foreign cities, and he shipped on a vessel bound to San Francisco.

This is a fine town, with a fine harbour, and rich people uncountable; and, in particular, there is one hill which is covered with palaces. Upon this hill Keawe was one day taking a walk, with his pocket full of money, viewing the great houses upon either hand with pleasure. 'What fine houses there are!' he was thinking, 'and how happy must these people be who dwell in them, and take care for the morrow!' The thought was in his mind when he came abreast of a house that was smaller than some others, but all finished and beautiful like a toy; the steps of that house shone like silver, and the borders of the garden bloomed like garlands, and the windows were bright like diamonds; and Keawe stopped and wondered at the excellence of all he saw. So stopping, he was aware of a man that looked forth upon him through a window, so clear that Keawe could see him as you see a fish in a pool upon the reef. The man was elderly, with a bald head and a black beard; and his face was heavy with sorrow, and he bitterly sighed. And the truth of it is, that as

Keawe looked in upon the man, and the man looked out upon Keawe, each envied the other.

All of a sudden the man smiled and nodded, and beckoned Keawe to enter, and met him at the door of the house.

'This is a fine house of mine,' said the man, and bitterly sighed. 'Would you not care to view the chambers?'

So he led Keawe all over it, from the cellar to the roof, and there was nothing there that was not perfect of its kind, and Keawe was astonished.

'Truly,' said Keawe, 'this is a beautiful house; if I lived in the like of it, I should be laughing all day long. How comes it, then, that you should be sighing?'

'There is no reason,' said the man, 'why you should not have a house in all points similar to this, and finer, if you wish. You have some money, I suppose?'

'I have fifty dollars,' said Keawe; 'but a house like this will cost more than fifty dollars.'

The man made a computation. 'I am sorry you have no more,' said he, 'for it may raise you trouble in the future; but it shall be yours at fifty dollars.'

'The house?' asked Keawe.

'No, not the house,' replied the man; 'but the bottle. For I must tell you, although I appear to you so rich and fortunate, all my fortune, and this house itself and its garden, came out of a bottle not much bigger than a pint. This is it.'

And he opened a lockfast place, and took out a round-bellied bottle with a long neck; the glass of it was white like milk, with changing rainbow colours in the grain. Within-sides something obscurely moved, like a shadow and a fire.

'This is thc bottle,' said the man; and, when Keawe laughed, 'You do not believe me?' he added. 'Try, then, for yourself. See if you can break it.'

So Keawe took the bottle up and dashed it on the

floor till he was weary; but it jumped on the floor like a child's ball, and was not injured.

'This is a strange thing,' said Keawe. 'For by the touch of it, as well as by the look, the bottle should be of glass.'

'Of glass it is,' replied the man, sighing more heavily than ever; 'but the glass of it was tempered in the flames of hell. An imp lives in it, and that is the shadow we behold there moving; or, so I suppose. If any man buy this bottle the imp is at his command; all that he desires—love, fame, money, houses like this house, aye, or a city like this city—all are his at the word uttered. Napoleon had this bottle, and by it he grew to be the king of the world; but he sold it at the last and fell. Captain Cook had this bottle, and by it he found his way to so many islands; but he too sold it, and was slain upon Hawaii. For, once it is sold, the power goes and the protection; and unless a man remain content with what he has, ill will befall him.'

'And yet you talk of selling it yourself?' Keawe said.

'I have all I wish, and I am growing elderly,' replied the man. 'There is one thing the imp cannot do—he cannot prolong life; and it would not be fair to conceal from you there is a drawback to the bottle; for if a man die before he sells it, he must burn in hell for ever.'

'To be sure, that is a drawback and no mistake,' cried Keawe. 'I would not meddle with the thing. I can do without a house, thank God; but there is one thing I could not be doing with one particle, and that is to be damned.'

'Dear me, you must not run away with things,' returned the man. 'All you have to do is to use the power of the imp in moderation, and then sell it to someone else, as I do to you, and finish your life in comfort.'

'Well, I observe two things,' said Keawe. 'All the

time you keep sighing like a maid in love—that is one; and for the other, you sell this bottle very cheap.'

'I have told you already why I sigh,' said the man. 'It is because I fear my health is breaking up; and, as you said yourself, to die and go to the devil is a pity for any one. As for why I sell so cheap, I must explain to you there is a peculiarity about the bottle. Long ago, when the devil brought it first upon earth, it was extremely expensive, and was sold first of all to Prester John for many millions of dollars; but it cannot be sold at all, unless sold at a loss. If you sell it for as much as you paid for it, back it comes to you again like a homing pigeon. It follows that the price has kept falling in these centuries, and the bottle is now remarkably cheap. I bought it myself from one of my great neighbours on this hill, and the price I paid was only ninety dollars. I could sell it for as high as eighty-nine dollars and ninety-nine cents, but not a penny dearer, or back the thing must come to me. Now, about this there are two bothers. First, when you offer a bottle so singular for eighty-odd dollars, people suppose you to be jesting. And second—but there is no hurry about that—and I need not go into it. Only remember it must be coined money that you sell it for.'

'How am I to know that this is all true?' asked Keawe.

'Some of it you can try at once,' replied the man. 'Give me your fifty dollars, take the bottle, and wish your fifty dollars back into your pocket. If that does not happen, I pledge you my honour I will cry off the bargain and restore your money.'

'You are not deceiving me?' said Keawe.

The man bound himself with a great oath.

'Well, I will risk that much,' said Keawe, 'for that can do no harm,' and he paid over his money to the man, and the man handed him the bottle.

'Imp of the bottle,' said Keawe, 'I want my fifty dollars back.' And sure enough, he had scarce said the word before his pocket was as heavy as ever.

'To be sure this is a wonderful bottle,' said Keawe.

'And now good-morning to you, my fine fellow, and the devil go with you for me,' said the man.

'Hold on,' said Keawe, 'I don't want any more of this fun. Here, take your bottle back.'

'You have bought it for less than I paid for it,' replied the man, rubbing his hands. 'It is yours now; and, for my part, I am only concerned to see the back of you.' And with that he rang for his Chinese servant, and had Keawe shown out of the house.

Now, when Keawe was in the street, with the bottle under his arm, he began to think. 'If all is true about this bottle, I may have made a losing bargain,' thinks he. 'But perhaps the man was only fooling me.' The first thing he did was to count his money; the sum was exact—forty-nine dollars, American money, and one Chili piece. 'That looks like the truth,' said Keawe. 'Now I will try another part.'

The streets in that part of the city were as clean as a ship's decks, and though it was noon, there were no passengers. Keawe set the bottle in the gutter and walked away. Twice he looked back, and there was the milky, round-bellied bottle where he left it. A third time, he looked back and turned a corner; but he had scarce done so, when something knocked upon his elbow, and behold! it was the long neck sticking up; and as for the round belly, it was jammed into the pocket of his pilot-coat.

'And that looks like the truth,' said Keawe.

The next thing he did was to buy a corkscrew in a shop, and go apart into a secret place in the fields. And there he tried to draw the cork, but as often as he put the screw in, out it came again, and the cork was as whole as ever.

'This is some new sort of cork,' said Keawe, and all at once he began to shake and sweat, for he was afraid of that bottle.

On his way back to the port-side he saw a shop where a man sold shells and clubs from the wild islands, old heathen deities, old coined money, pictures from China and Japan, and all manner of things that sailors bring in their sea-chests. And here he had an idea. So he went in and offered the bottle for a hundred dollars. The man of the shop laughed at him at first, and offered him five; but, indeed, it was a curious bottle, such glass was never blown in any human glassworks, so prettily the colours shone under the milky white, and so strangely the shadow hovered in the midst; so, after he had disputed a while after the manner of his kind, the shopman gave Keawe sixty silver dollars for the thing and set it on a shelf in the midst of his window.

'Now,' said Keawe, 'I have sold that for sixty which I bought for fifty—or, to say truth, a little less, because one of my dollars was from Chili. Now I shall know the truth upon another point.'

So he went back on board his ship, and when he opened his chest, there was the bottle, which had come more quickly than himself. Now Keawe had a mate on board whose name was Lopaka.

'What ails you,' said Lopaka, 'that you stare in your chest?'

They were alone in the ship's forecastle, and Keawe bound him to secrecy, and told all.

'This is a very strange affair,' said Lopaka; 'and I fear you will be in trouble about this bottle. But there is one point very clear—that you are sure of the trouble, and you had better have the profit in the bargain. Make up your mind what you want with it; give the order, and if it is done as you desire, I will buy the bottle myself; for I have an idea of my own to get a schooner, and go trading through the islands.'

'That is not my idea,' said Keawe; 'but to have a beautiful house and garden on the Kona coast, where I was born, the sun shining in at the door, flowers in the garden, glass in the windows, pictures on the walls, and toys and fine carpets on the tables, for all the world like the house I was in this day—only a storey higher, and with balconies all about like the king's palace; and to live there without care and make merry with my friends and relatives.'

'Well,' said Lopaka, 'let us carry it back with us to Hawaii; and if all comes true as you suppose, I will buy the bottle, as I said, and ask a schooner.'

Upon that they were agreed, and it was not long before the ship returned to Honolulu, carrying Keawe and Lopaka, and the bottle. They were scarce come ashore when they met a friend upon the beach, who began at once to condole with Keawe.

'I do not know what I am to be condoled about,' said Keawe.

'Is it possible you have not heard,' said the friend, 'your uncle—that good old man—is dead, and your cousin—that beautiful boy—was drowned at sea?'

Keawe was filled with sorrow, and, beginning to weep and to lament, he forgot about the bottle. But Lopaka was thinking to himself, and presently, when Keawe's grief was a little abated, 'I have been thinking,' said Lopaka, 'had not your uncle lands in Hawaii, in the district of Kaü?'

'No,' said Keawe, 'not in Kaü: they are on the mountainside—a little be-south Hookena.'

'These lands will now be yours?' asked Lopaka.

'And so they will,' says Keawe, and began again to lament for his relatives.

'No,' said Lopaka, 'do not lament at present. I have a thought in my mind. How if this should be the doing of the bottle? For here is the place ready for your house.'

'If this be so,' cried Keawe, 'it is a very ill way to serve me by killing my relatives. But it may be, indeed; for it was in just a station that I saw the house with my mind's eye.'

'The house, however, is not yet built,' said Lopaka.

'No, not like to be!' said Keawe; 'for though my uncle has some coffee and ava and bananas, it will not be more than will keep me in comfort; and the rest of that land is the black lava.'

'Let us go to the lawyer,' said Lopaka; 'I have still this idea in my mind.'

Now, when they came to the lawyer's, it appeared Keawe's uncle had grown monstrous rich in the last days, and there was a fund of money.

'And here is the money for the house!' cried Lopaka.

'If you are thinking of a new house,' said the lawyer, 'here is the card of a new architect of whom they tell me great things.'

'Better and better!' cried Lopaka. 'Here is all made plain for us. Let us continue to obey orders.'

So they went to the architect, and he had drawings of houses on his table.

'You want something out of the way,' said the architect. 'How do you like this?' and he handed a drawing to Keawe.

Now, when Keawe set eyes on the drawing, he cried out aloud, for it was the picture of his thought exactly drawn.

'I am in for this house,' thought he. 'Little as I like the way it comes to me, I am in for it now, and I may as well take the good along with the evil.'

So he told the architect all that he wished, and how he would have that house furnished, and about the pictures on the walls and the knick-knacks on the tables; and he asked the man plainly for how much he would undertake the whole affair.

The architect put many questions, and took his pen and made a computation; and when he had done he named the very sum that Keawe had inherited.

Lopaka and Keawe looked at one another and nodded.

'It is quite clear,' thought Keawe, 'that I am to have this house, whether or no. It comes from the devil, and I fear I will get little good by that; and of one thing I am sure, I will make no more wishes as long as I have this bottle. But with the house I am saddled, and I may as well take the good along with the evil.'

So he made his terms with the architect, and they signed a paper; and Keawe and Lopaka took ship again and sailed to Australia; for it was concluded between them they should not interfere at all, but leave the architect and the bottle imp to build and to adorn the house at their own pleasure.

The voyage was a good voyage, only all the time Keawe was holding in his breath, for he had sworn he would utter no more wishes, and take no more favours from the devil. The time was up when they got back. The architect told them that the house was ready, and Keawe and Lopaka took a passage in the *Hall*, and went down Kona way to view the house, and see if all had been done fitly according to the thought that was in Keawe's mind.

Now, the house stood on the mountain-side, visible to ships. Above, the forest ran up into the clouds of rain: below, the black lava fell in cliffs, where the kings of old lay buried. A garden bloomed about the house with every hue of flowers; and there was an orchard of papaia on the one hand and an orchard of bread-fruit on the other, and right in front, towards the sea, a ship's mast had been rigged up and bore a flag. As for the house, it was three storeys high, with great chambers and broad balconies on each. The windows were of glass, so excellent that it was as clear as water and as bright as day. All manner of furniture adorned the chambers. Pictures hung upon the wall in golden frames—pictures of ships, and men fighting, and of the most beautiful women, and of singular places; nowhere in the world are there pictures of so bright a colour as those Keawe found hanging in his house. As for the knick-knacks they were extraordinarily fine: chiming clocks and musical boxes, little men with nodding heads, books filled with pictures, weapons of price from all quarters of the world, and the most elegant puzzles to entertain the leisure of a solitary man. And as no one would care to live in such chambers, only to walk through and view them, the balconies were made so broad that a whole town might have lived upon them in delight; and Keawe knew not which to prefer, whether the back porch, where you get the land breeze and looked upon the orchards and the flowers, or the front balcony, where you could drink the wind of the sea, and look down the steep wall of the mountain and see the *Hall* going by once a week or so between Hookena and the hills of Pele, or the schooners plying up the coast for wood and ava and bananas.

When they had viewed all, Keawe and Lopaka sat on the porch.

'Well,' asked Lopaka, 'is it all as you designed?'

'Words cannot utter it,' said Keawe. 'It is better than I dreamed, and I am sick with satisfaction.'

'There is but one thing to consider,' said Lopaka; 'all this may be quite natural, and the bottle imp have nothing whatever to say to it. If I were to buy the bottle, and got no schooner after all, I should have put my hand in the fire for nothing. I gave you my word, I know; but yet I think you would not grudge me one more proof.'

'I have sworn I would take no more favours,' said Keawe. 'I have gone already deep enough.'

'This is no favour I am thinking of,' replied Lopaka. 'It is only to see the imp himself. There is nothing to be gained by that, and so nothing to be ashamed of, and yet, if I once saw him, I should be sure of the whole matter. So indulge me so far, and let me see the imp; and, after that, here is the money in my hand, and I will buy it.'

'There is only one thing I am afraid of,' said Keawe. 'The imp may be very ugly to view, and if you once set eyes upon him you might be very undesirous of the bottle.'

'I am a man of my word,' said Lopaka. 'And here is the money betwixt us.'

'Very well,' replied Keawe, 'I have a curiosity myself. So come, let us have one look at you, Mr Imp.'

Now as soon as that was said, the imp looked out of the bottle, and in again, swift as a lizard; and there saw Keawe and Lopaka turned to stone. The night had quite come, before either found a thought to say or voice to say it with; and then Lopaka pushed the money over and took the bottle.

'I am a man of my word,' said he, 'and had need to be so, or I would not touch this bottle with my foot. Well, I shall get my schooner and a dollar or two for my pocket; and then I will be rid of this devil as fast as I can. For to tell you the plain truth, the look of him has cast me down.'

'Lopaka,' said Keawe, 'do not you think any worse of me than you can help; I know it is night, and the roads bad, and the pass by the tombs an ill place to go by so late, but I declare since I have seen that little face, I cannot eat or sleep or pray till it is gone from me. I will give you a lantern, and a basket to put the bottle in, and any picture or fine thing in all my house that takes your fancy; and be gone at once, and go sleep at Hookena with Nahinu.'

'Keawe,' said Lopaka, 'many a man would take this ill; above all, when I am doing you a turn so friendly, as to keep my word and buy the bottle; and for that matter, the night and the dark, and the way by the tombs, must be all tenfold more dangerous to a man with such a sin upon his conscience and such a bottle under his arm. But for my part, I am so extremely terrified myself, I have not the heart to blame you. Here I go, then; and I pray God you may be happy in your house, and I fortunate with my schooner, and both get to heaven in the end in spite of the devil and his bottle.'

So Lopaka went down the mountain; and Keawe stood in his front balcony, and listened to the clink of the horse's shoes, and watched the lantern go shining down the path, and along the cliff of caves where the old dead are buried; and all the time he trembled and clasped his hands, and prayed for his friend, and gave glory to God that he himself was escaped out of that trouble.

But the next day came very brightly, and that new house of his was so delightful to behold that he forgot his terrors. One day followed another, and Keawe dwelt there in perpetual joy. He had his place on the back porch; it was there he ate and lived, and read the stories in the Honolulu newspapers; but when any one came by they would go in and view the chambers and the pictures. And the fame of the house went far and wide; it was called *Ka-Hale Nui*—the Great House—in all Kona; and sometimes the Bright House, for Keawe kept a Chinaman, who was all day dusting and furbishing; and the glass, and the gilt, and the fine stuffs, and the pictures, shone as bright as the morning. As for Keawe himself, he could not walk in the chambers without singing, his heart was so enlarged; and when ships sailed by upon the sea, he would fly his colours on the mast.

So time went by, until one day Keawe went upon a visit as far as Kailua to certain of his friends. There he was well feasted; and left as soon as he could the next morning, and rode hard, for he was impatient to behold his beautiful house; and, besides, the night then coming on was the night in which the dead old days go abroad in the sides of Kona; and having already meddled with the devil, he was the more chary of meeting with the dead. A little beyond Honaunau, looking far ahead, he was aware of a woman bathing in the edges of the sea; and she seemed a well-grown girl, but he thought no more of it. Then he saw her white shift flutter as she put it on, and then her red holoku; and by the time he came abreast of her she was done with her toilet, and had come up from the sea, and stood by the trackside in her red holoku, and she was all freshened with the bath, and her eyes shone and were kind. Now Keawe no sooner beheld her than he drew rein.

'I thought I knew every one in this country,' said he. 'How comes it that I do not know you?'

'I am Kokua, daughter of Kiano,' said the girl, 'and I have just returned from Oahu. Who are you?'

'I will tell you who I am in a little,' said Keawe, dismounting from his horse, 'but not now. For I have a thought in my mind, and if you knew who I was, you might have heard of me, and would not give me a true answer. But tell me, first of all, one thing: are you married?'

At this Kokua laughed out aloud. 'It is you who ask questions,' she said. 'Are you married yourself?'

'Indeed, Kokua, I am not,' replied Keawe, 'and never thought to be until this hour. But here is the plain truth. I have met you here at the roadside, and I saw your eyes, which are like the stars, and my heart went to you as swift as a bird. And so now, if you want none of me, say so and I will go on to my own place; but if you think me no worse than any other young man, say so, too, and I will turn aside to your father's for the night, and tomorrow I will talk with the good man.'

Kokua said never a word, but she looked at the sea and laughed.

'Kokua,' said Keawe, 'if you say nothing, I will take that for the good answer; so let us be stepping to your father's door.'

She went on ahead of him, still without speech; only sometimes she glanced back and glanced away again, and she kept the strings of her hat in her mouth.

Now, when they had come to the door, Kiano came out on his veranda, and cried out and welcomed Keawe by name. At that the girl looked over, for the fame of the great house had come to her ears; and, to be sure, it was a great temptation. All that evening, they were very merry together; and the girl was as bold as brass under the eyes of her parents, and made a mark of Keawe, for she had a quick wit. The next day he had a word with Kiano, and found the girl alone.

'Kokua,' said he, 'you made a mark of me all the evening and it is still time to bid me go. I would not tell you who I was, because I have so fine a house, and I feared you would think too much of that house and too little of the man that loves you. Now you know all, and if you wish to have seen the last of me, say so at once.'

'No,' said Kokua, but this time she did not laugh, nor did Keawe ask for more.

This was the wooing of Keawe; things had gone quickly; but so an arrow goes, and the ball of a rifle swifter still, and yet both may strike the target. Things had gone fast, but they had gone far also, and the thought of Keawe rang in the maiden's head; she heard his voice in the breach of the surf upon the lava, and for this young man that she had seen but twice she would have left father and mother and her native islands. As for Keawe himself, his horse flew up the path of the mountain under the cliff of tombs, and the sound of the hoofs, and the sound of Keawe singing to himself for pleasure, echoed in the caverns of the dead.

He came to the Bright House, and still he was singing. He sat and ate in the broad balcony, and the Chinaman wondered at his master, to hear how he sang between the mouthfuls. The sun went down into the sea, and the night came; and Keawe walked the balconies by lamplight, high on the mountains, and the voice of his singing started men on ships.

'Here am I now upon my high place,' he said to himself. 'Life may be no better; this is the mountain top; and all shelves about me towards the worse. For the first time I will light up the chambers, and bathe in my fine bath with the hot water and the cold, and sleep above in the bed of my bridal chamber.'

So the Chinaman had word, and he must rise from sleep and light the furnaces; and as he walked below, beside the boilers, he heard his master singing and rejoicing above him in the lighted chambers. When the water began to be hot the Chinaman cried to his master: and Keawe went into the bathroom; and the Chinaman heard him sing as he filled the marble basin; and heard him sing, and the singing broken, as he undressed; until of a sudden, the song ceased. The Chinaman listened, and listened; he called up the house to Keawe to ask if all were well, and Keawe answered him 'Yes', and bade him go to bed; but there was no more singing in the Bright House; and all night long the Chinaman heard his master's feet go round and round the balconies without repose.

Now, the truth of it was this: as Keawe undressed for his bath, he spied upon his flesh a patch like a patch of lichen on a rock, and it was then that he stopped singing. For he knew the likeness of that patch, and knew that he was fallen in the Chinese Evil.*

Now, it is a sad thing for any man to fall into this sickness. And it would be a sad thing for any one to leave a house so beautiful and so commodious; and

* Leprosy

depart from all his friends to the north coast of Molokai, between the mighty cliff and the sea-breakers. But what was that to the case of the man Keawe, he who had met his love but yesterday and won her but that morning, and now saw all his hopes break, in a moment, like a piece of glass?

A while he sat upon the edge of the bath, then sprang, with a cry, and ran outside and to and fro, to and fro, along the balcony, like one despairing.

'Very willingly could I leave Hawaii, the home of my fathers,' Keawe was thinking. 'Very lightly could I leave my house, the high-placed, the many-windowed, here upon the mountains. Very bravely could I go to Molokai, to Kalaupapa by the cliffs, to live with the smitten and to sleep there, far from my fathers. But what wrong have I done, what sin lies upon my soul, that I should have encountered Kokua coming cool from the sea-water in the evening? Kokua, the soul-ensnarer! Kokua, the light of my life! Her may I never wed, her may I look upon no longer, her may I no more handle with my loving hand and it is for this, it is for you, O Kokua! that I pour my lamentations!'

Now you are to observe what sort of a man Keawe was, for he might have dwelt there in the Bright House for years, and no one been the wiser of his sickness; but he reckoned nothing of that, if he must lose Kokua. And again he might have wed Kokua even as he was; and so many would have done, because they have the souls of pigs; but Keawe loved the maiden manfully, and he would do her no hurt and bring her in no danger.

A little beyond the midst of the night, there came in his mind the recollection of that bottle. He went round to the back porch, and called to memory the day when the devil had looked forth; and at the thought ice ran in his veins.

'A dreadful thing is the bottle,' thought Keawe, 'and dreadful is the imp, and it is a dreadful thing to risk the flames of hell. But what other hope have I to cure my sickness or to wed Kokua! What!' he thought, 'would I beard the devil once, only to get me a house, and not face him again to win Kokua?'

Thereupon he called to mind it was the next day the *Hall* went by on her return to Honolulu. 'There must I go first,' he thought, 'and see Lopaka. For the best hope that I have now is to find that same bottle I was so pleased to be rid of.'

Never a wink could he sleep; the food stuck in his throat; but he sent a letter to Kiano, and about the time when the steamer would be coming, rode down beside the cliff of the tombs. It rained; his horse went heavily; he looked up at the black mouths of the caves, and he envied the dead that slept there and were done with trouble; and called to mind how he had galloped by the day before, and was astonished. So he came down to Hookena, and there was all the country gathered for the steamer as usual. In the shed before the store they sat and rested and passed the news; but there was no matter of speech in Keawe's bosom, and he sat in their midst and looked without on the rain falling on the houses, and the surf beating among the rocks, and the sighs arose in his throat.

'Keawe of the Bright House is out of spirits,' said one to another. Indeed, and so he was, and little wonder.

Then the *Hall* came, and the whale-boat carried him on board. The after-part of the ship was full of *Haoles** —who had been to visit the volcano, as their custom is; and the midst was crowned with Kanakas, and the forepart with wild bulls from Hilo and horses from Kaü; but Keawe sat apart from all in his sorrow, and watched for the house of Kiano. There it sat low upon the shore in the black rocks, and shaded by the cocoa-palms, and there by the door was a red holoku,

* Whites

no greater than a fly, and going to and fro with a fly's busyness. 'Ah, queen of my heart,' he cried, 'I'll venture my dear soul to win you!'

Soon after darkness fell and the cabins were lit up, and the Haoles sat and played at the cards and drank whisky as their custom is; but Keawe walked the deck all night; and all the next day, as they steamed under the lee of Maui or of Molokai, he was still pacing to and fro like a wild animal in a menagerie.

Towards evening they passed Diamond Head, and came to the pier of Honolulu. Keawe stepped out among the crowd and began to ask for Lopaka. It seemed he had become the owner of a schooner—none better in the islands—and was gone upon an adventure as far as Pola-Pola or Kahiki; so there was no help to be looked for from Lopaka. Keawe called to mind a friend of his, a lawyer in the town (I must not tell his name), and inquired of him. They said he was grown suddenly rich, and had a fine new house upon Waikiki shore; and this put a thought in Keawe's head, and he called a hack and drove to the lawyer's house.

The house was all brand new, and the trees in the garden no greater than walking-sticks, and the lawyer, when he came, had the air of a man well pleased.

'What can I do to serve you?' said the lawyer.

'You are a friend of Lopaka's,' replied Keawe, 'and Lopaka purchased from me a certain piece of goods that I thought you might enable me to trace.'

The lawyer's face became very dark. 'I do not profess to misunderstand you, Mr Keawe,' said he, 'though this is an ugly business to be stirring in. You may be sure I know nothing, but yet I have a guess, and if you would apply in a certain quarter I think you might have news.'

And he named the name of a man, which, again, I had better not repeat. So it was for days, and Keawe went from one to another, finding everywhere new clothes and carriages, and fine new houses, and men everywhere in great contentment, although, to be sure, when he hinted at his business their faces would cloud over.

'No doubt I am upon the track,' thought Keawe. 'These new clothes and carriages are all the gifts of the little imp, and these glad faces are the faces of men who had taken their profit and got rid of the accursed thing in safety. When I see pale cheeks and hear sighing, I shall know that I am near the bottle.'

So it befell at last he was recommended to a Haole in Beritania Street. When he came to the door, about the hour of the evening meal, there were the usual marks of the new house, and the young garden, and the electric light shining in the windows; but when the owner came, a shock of hope and fear ran through Keawe; for here was a young man, white as a corpse, and black about the eyes, the hair shedding from his head, and such a look in his countenance as a man may have when he is waiting for the gallows.

'Here it is, to be sure,' thought Keawe, and so with this man he noways veiled his errand. 'I am come to buy the bottle,' said he.

At the word, the young Haole of Beritania Street reeled against the wall.

'The bottle!' he gasped. 'To buy the bottle!' Then he seemed to choke, and seizing Keawe by the arm, carried him into a room and poured out wine in two glasses.

'Here is my respects,' said Keawe, who had been much about with Haoles in his time. 'Yes,' he added, 'I am come to buy the bottle. What is the price by now?'

At that word the young man let his glass slip through his fingers, and looked upon Keawe like a ghost.

'The price,' says he; 'the price! You do not know the price?'

'It is for that I am asking you,' returned Keawe. 'But why are you so much concerned? Is there anything wrong about the price?'

'It has dropped a great deal in value since your time, Mr Keawe,' said the young man, stammering.

'Well, well, I shall have the less to pay for it,' says Keawe. 'How much did it cost you?'

The young man was as white as a sheet. 'Two cents,' said he.

'What!' cried Keawe, 'two cents? Why, then, you can only sell it for one. And he who buys it—' The words died upon Keawe's tongue; he who bought it could never sell it again, the bottle and the bottle imp must abide with him until he died, and when he died must carry him to the red end of hell.

The young man of Beritania Street fell upon his knees. 'For God's sake, buy it!' he cried. 'You can have all my fortune in the bargain. I was mad when I bought it at that price. I had embezzled money at my store; I was lost else; I must have gone to jail.'

'Poor creature,' said Keawe, 'you would risk your soul upon so desperate an adventure, and to avoid the proper punishment of your own disgrace; and you think I could hesitate with love in front of me. Give me the bottle, and the change which I make sure you have all ready. Here is a five-cent piece.'

It was as Keawe supposed; the young man had the change ready in a drawer; the bottle changed hands, and Keawe's fingers were no sooner clasped upon the stalk than he had breathed his wish to be a clean man. And sure enough, when he got home to his room, and stripped himself before a glass his flesh was whole like an infant's. And here was the strange thing; he had no sooner seen this miracle than his mind was changed within him, and he cared naught for the Chinese Evil, and little enough for Kokua; and had but the one thought, that here he was bound to the bottle imp for time and for eternity, and had no better hope but to be a cinder for ever in the flames of hell. Away ahead of him he saw them blaze with his mind's eye, and his soul shrank, and darkness fell upon the light.

When Keawe came to himself a little, he was aware it was the night when the band played at the hotel. Thither he went, because he feared to be alone; and there, among happy faces, walked to and fro, and heard the tunes go up and down, and saw Berger beat the measure, and all the while he heard the flames crackle and saw the red fire burning in the bottomless pit. Of a sudden the band played *Hiki-ao-ao*; that was a song that he had sung with Kokua, and at the strain courage returned to him.

'It is done now,' he thought, 'and once more let me take the good along with the evil.'

So it befell that he returned to Hawaii by the first steamer, and as soon as it could be managed he was wedded to Kokua, and carried her up the mountain-side to the Bright House.

Now it was so with these two, that when they were together Keawe's heart was stilled; but as soon as he was alone he fell into a brooding horror, and heard the flames crackle, and saw the red fire burn in the bottomless pit. The girl, indeed, had come to him wholly; her heart leaped in her side at sight of him, her hand clung to his; and she was so fashioned, from the hair upon her head to the nails upon her toes, that none could see her without joy. She was pleasant in her nature. She had the good word always. Full of song she was, and went to and fro in the Bright House, the brightest thing in its three storeys, carolling like the birds. And Keawe beheld and heard her with delight, and then must shrink upon one side, and weep and groan to think upon the price that he had paid for her; and then he must dry his eyes and wash his face, and go and sit with her on the broad balconies, joining in her songs, and, with a sick spirit, answering her smiles.

There came a day when her feet began to be heavy

and her songs more rare; and now it was not Keawe only that would weep apart, but each would sunder from the other and sit in opposite balconies with the whole width of the Bright House betwixt. Keawe was so sunk in his despair he scarce observed the change, and was only glad he had more hours to sit alone and brood upon his destiny, and was not so frequently condemned to pull a smiling face on a sick heart. But one day, coming softly through the house, he heard the sound of a child sobbing, and there was Kokua rolling her face upon the balcony floor, and weeping like the lost.

'You do well to weep in this house, Kokua,' he said. 'And yet I would give the head off my body that you (at least) might have been happy.'

'Happy!' she cried. 'Keawe, when you lived alone in your Bright House you were the word of the island for a happy man; laughter and song were in your mouth, and your face was as bright as the sunrise. Then you wedded poor Kokua; and the good God knows what is amiss in her—but from that day you have not smiled. Oh!' she cried, 'what ails me? I thought I was pretty, and I knew I loved him. What ails me, that I throw this cloud upon my husband?'

'Poor Kokua,' said Keawe. He sat down by her side, and sought to take her hand; but that she plucked away. 'Poor Kokua,' he said again. 'My poor child—my pretty. And I had thought all this while to spare you! Well, you shall know all. Then, at least, you will pity poor Keawe; then you will understand how much he loved you in the past—that he dared hell for your possession—and how much he loves you still (the poor condemned one), that he can yet call up a smile when he beholds you.'

With that he told her all, even from the beginning.

'You have done this for me?' she cried. 'Ah, well,

then what do I care!' and she clasped and wept upon him.

'Ah, child!' said Keawe, 'and yet, when I consider of the fire of hell, I care a good deal!'

'Never tell me,' said she, 'no man can be lost because he loved Kokua, and no other fault. I tell you, Keawe, I shall save you with these hands, or perish in your company. What? you loved me and gave your soul, and you think I will not die to save you in return?'

'Ah, my dear, you might die a hundred times: and what difference would that make?' he cried, 'except to leave me lonely till the time comes for my damnation?'

'You know nothing,' said she. 'I was educated in a school in Honolulu; I am no common girl. And I tell you I shall save my lover. What is this you say about a cent? But all the world is not American. In England they have a piece they call a farthing, which is about half a cent. Ah! sorrow!' she cried, 'that makes it scarcely better, for the buyer must be lost, and we shall find none so brave as my Keawe! But then, there is France; they have a small coin there which they call a centime, and these go five to the cent, or thereabout. We could not do better. Come, Keawe, let us go to the French islands; let us go to Tahiti, as fast as ships can bear us. There we have four centimes, three centimes, two centimes, one centime; four possible sales to come and go on; and two of us to push the bargain. Come, my Keawe! kiss me, and banish care. Kokua will defend you.'

'Gift of God!' he cried. 'I cannnot think that God will punish me for desiring aught so good. Be it as you will, then, take me where you please; I put my life and my salvation in your hands.'

Early the next day Kokua went about her preparations. She took Keawe's chest that he went with sailoring; and first she put the bottle in a corner, and then packed it with the richest of their clothes and the bravest of the knick-knacks in the house. 'For,' said she, 'we must seem to be rich folks, or who would believe in the bottle?' All the time of her preparation she was as gay as a bird; only when she looked upon Keawe the tears would spring in her eyes, and she must run and kiss him. As for Keawe, a weight was off his soul; now that he had his secret shared, and some hope in front of him he seemed like a new man; his feet went lightly on the earth, and his breath was good to him again. Yet was terror still at his elbow; and ever and again, as the wind blows out a taper, hope died in him, and he saw the flame toss and the red fire burn in hell.

It was given out in the country they were gone pleasuring in the States, which was thought a strange thing, and yet not so strange as the truth, if any could have guessed it. So they went to Honolulu in the *Hall*, and thence in the *Umatilla* to San Francisco with a crowd of Haoles, and at San Francisco took their passage by the mail brigantine, the *Tropic Bird*, for Papeete, the chief place of the French in the south islands. Thither they came, after a pleasant voyage, on a fair day of the Trade Wind, and saw the reef with the surf breaking and Motuiti with its palms, and the schooner riding withinside, and the white houses of the town low down along the shore among green trees, and overhead the mountains and the clouds of Tahiti, the wise island.

It was judged the most wise to hire a house, which they did accordingly, opposite the British Consul's, to make a great parade of money, and themselves conspicuous with carriages and horses. This it was very easy to do so long as they had the bottle in their possession; for Kokua was more bold than Keawe, and, whenever she had a mind, called on the imp for twenty or a hundred dollars. At this rate they soon grew to be remarked in the town; and the strangers from Hawaii, their riding and their driving, the fine holokus, and the rich lace of Kokua, became the matter of much talk.

They got on well after the first with the Tahitian language, which is indeed like to the Hawaiian, with a change of certain letters; and as soon as they had any freedom of speech, began to push the bottle. You are to consider it was not an easy subject to introduce; it is not easy to persuade people you are in earnest, when you offer to sell them for four centimes the spring of health and riches inexhaustible. It was necessary, besides, to explain the dangers of the bottle; and either people disbelieved the whole thing and laughed, or they thought the more of the darker part, became overcast with gravity, and drew away from Keawe and Kokua, as from persons who had dealings with the devil. So far from gaining ground, these two began to find they were avoided in the town; the children ran away from them screaming, a thing intolerable to Kokua; Catholics crossed themselves as they went by; and all persons began with one accord to disengage themselves from their advances.

Depression fell upon their spirits. They would sit at night in their new house, after a day's weariness, and not exchange one word or the silence would be broken by Kokua bursting suddenly into sobs. Sometimes they would pray together; sometimes they would have the bottle out upon the floor, and sit all evening watching how the shadow hovered in the midst. At such times they would be afraid to go to rest. It was long ere slumber came to them, and, if either dozed off, it would be to wake and find the other silently weeping in the dark, or, perhaps, to wake alone, the other having fled from the house and the neighbourhood of that bottle, to pace under the bananas in the little garden, or to wander on the beach by moonlight.

One night it was so when Kokua awoke. Keawe

was gone. She felt in the bed and his place was cold. Then fear fell upon her, and she sat up in bed. A little moonshine filtered through the shutters. The room was bright, and she could spy the bottle on the floor. Outside it blew high, the great trees of the avenues cried aloud, and the fallen leaves rattled in the veranda. In the midst of this Kokua was aware of another sound; whether of a beast or of a man she could scarce tell, but it was as sad as death, and cut her to the soul. Softly she arose, set the door ajar, and looked forth into the moonlit yard. There, under the bananas, lay Keawe, his mouth in the dust, and as he lay he moaned.

It was Kokua's first thought to run forward and console him; her second potently withheld her. Keawe had borne himself before his wife like a brave man; it became her little in the hour of weakness to intrude upon his shame. With the thought she drew back into the house.

'Heaven,' she thought, 'how careless have I been—how weak! It is he, not I that stands in this eternal peril; it was he, not I, that took the curse upon his soul. It is for my sake, and for the love of a creature of so little worth and such poor help, that he now beholds so close to him the flames of hell—aye, and smells the smoke of it, lying without there in the wind and moonlight. Am I so dull of spirit that never till now have I surmised my duty, or have I seen it before and turned aside? But now, at least, I take up my soul in both the hands of my affection; now I say farewell to the white steps of heaven and the waiting faces of my friends. A love for a love, and let mine be equalled with Keawe's! A soul for a soul, and be it mine to punish!'

She was a deft woman with her hands, and was soon apparelled. She took in her hands the change—the precious centimes they kept ever at their side; for this coin is little used, and they had made provision at a government office. When she was forth in the avenue clouds came on the wind, and the moon was blackened. The town slept, and she knew not whither to turn till she heard one coughing in the shadow of the trees.

'Old man,' said Kokua, 'what do you here abroad in the cold night?'

The old man could scarce express himself for coughing, but she made out that he was old and poor, and a stranger in the island.

'Will you do me a service?' said Kokua. 'As one stranger to another, and as an old man to a young woman, will you help a daughter of Hawaii?'

'Ah,' said the old man. 'So you are the witch from the Eight Islands, and even my old soul you seek to entangle. But I have heard of you, and defy your wickedness.'

'Sit down here,' said Kokua, 'and let me tell you a tale.' And she told him the story of Keawe from the beginning to the end.

'And now,' said she, 'I am his wife, whom he bought with his soul's welfare. And what should I do? If I went to him myself and offered to buy it, he will refuse. But if you go, he will sell it eagerly; I will await you here; you will buy it for four centimes, and I will buy it again for three. And the Lord strengthen a poor girl!'

'If you meant falsely,' said the old man, 'I think God would strike you dead.'

'He would!' cried Kokua. 'Be sure He would. I could not be so treacherous; God would not suffer it.'

'Give me the four centimes and await me here,' said the old man.

Now, when Kokua stood alone in the street, her spirit died. The wind roared in the trees, and it seemed to her the rushing of the flames of hell; the shadows towered in the light of the street lamp, and they seemed to her the snatching hands of evil ones. If she had had the strength, she must have run away, and if she had had the breath, she must have screamed aloud; but, in truth, she could do neither, and stood and trembled in the avenue, like an affrighted child.

Then she saw the old man returning, and he had the bottle in his hand.

'I have done your bidding,' said he. 'I left your husband weeping like a child; tonight he will sleep easy.' And he held the bottle forth.

'Before you give it me,' Kokua panted, 'take the good with the evil—ask to be delivered from your cough.'

'I am an old man,' replied the other, 'and too near the gate of the grave to take a favour from the devil. But what is this? Why do you not take the bottle? Do you hesitate?'

'Not hesitate!' cried Kokua. 'I am only weak. Give me a moment. It is my hand resists, my flesh shrinks back from the accursed thing. One moment only!'

The old man looked upon Kokua kindly. 'Poor child!' said he, 'you fear: your soul misgives you. Well, let me keep it. I am old, and can never more be happy in this world, and as for the next . . .'

'Give it me!' gasped Kokua. 'There is your money. Do you think I am so base as that? Give me the bottle.'

'God bless you, child,' said the old man.

Kokua concealed the bottle under her holoku, said farewell to the old man, and walked off along the avenue, she cared not whither. For all roads were now the same to her, and led equally to hell. Sometimes she walked, and sometimes ran; sometimes she screamed out loud in the night, and sometimes lay by the wayside in the dust and wept. All that she had heard of hell came back to her; she saw the flames blaze, and she smelled the smoke, and her flesh withered on the coals.

Near day she came to her mind again, and returned to

the house. It was even as the old man said—Keawe slumbered like a child. Kokua stood and gazed upon his face.

'Now, my husband,' said she, 'it is your turn to sleep. When you wake it will be your turn to sing and laugh. But for poor Kokua, alas! that meant no evil—for poor Kokua no more sleep, no more singing, no more delight, whether in earth or heaven.'

With that she lay down in the bed by his side, and her misery was so extreme that she fell in a deep slumber instantly.

Late in the morning her husband woke her and gave her the good news. It seemed he was silly with delight, for he paid no heed to her distress, ill though she dissembled it. The words stuck in her mouth; it mattered not, Keawe did the speaking. She ate not a bite, but who was to observe it? For Keawe cleared the dish. Kokua saw and heard him, like some strange thing in a dream; there were times when she forgot or doubted, and put her hands to her brow; to know herself doomed and hear her husband's babble, seemed so monstrous.

All the while Keawe was eating and talking, and planning the time of their return, and thanking her for saving him and fondling her, and calling her the true helper after all. He laughed at the old man that was fool enough to buy that bottle.

'A worthy old man he seemed,' Keawe said. 'But no one can judge by appearances. For why did the old reprobate require the bottle?'

'My husband,' said Kokua humbly, 'his purpose may have been good.'

Keawe laughed like an angry man.

'Fiddle-de-dee!' cried Keawe. 'An old rogue, I tell you; and an old ass to boot. For the bottle was hard enough to sell at four centimes; and at three it will be quite impossible. The margin is not broad enough, the thing begins to smell of scorching—brrr!' said he, and shuddered. 'It is true I bought it myself at a cent, when I knew not there were smaller coins. I was a fool for my pains; there will never be found another, and whoever has that bottle now will carry it to the pit.'

'O my husband!' said Kokua. 'Is it not a terrible thing to save oneself by the eternal ruin of another? It seems to me I could not laugh. I would be humbled. I would be filled with melancholy. I would pray for the poor holder.'

Then Keawe, because he felt the truth of what she said, grew the more angry. 'Heighty-teighty!' cried he. 'You may be filled with melancholy if you please. It is not the mind of a good wife. If you thought at all of me, you would sit shamed.'

Thereupon he went out, and Kokua was alone.

What chance had she to sell that bottle at two centimes? None, she perceived. And if she had any, here was her husband hurrying her away to a country where there was nothing lower than a cent. And here—on the morrow of her sacrifice—was her husband leaving her and blaming her.

She would not even try to profit by what time she had, but sat in the house, and now had the bottle out and viewed it with unutterable fear, and now, with loathing, hid it out of sight.

By-and-by Keawe came back, and would have her take a drive.

'My husband, I am ill,' she said. 'I am out of heart. Excuse me, I can take no pleasure.'

Then was Keawe more wroth than ever. With her, because he thought she was brooding over the case of the old man; and with himself, because he thought she was right and was ashamed to be so happy.

'This is your truth,' cried he, 'and this your affection! Your husband is just saved from eternal ruin, which he encountered for the love of you—and you can take no pleasure! Kokua, you have a disloyal heart.'

He went forth again furious, and wandered in the town all day. He met friends, and drank with them; they hired a carriage and drove into the country, and there drank again. All the time Keawe was ill at ease, because he was taking this pastime while his wife was sad, and because he knew in his heart that she was more right than he; and the knowledge made him drink the deeper.

Now there was an old brutal Haole drinking with him, one that had been a boatswain of a whaler—a runaway, a digger in gold mines, a convict in prisons. He had a low mind and a foul mouth; he loved to drink and to see others drunken; and he pressed the glass upon Keawe. Soon there was no more money in the company.

'Here you!' says the boatswain, 'you are rich, you have been always saying. You have a bottle or some foolishness.'

'Yes,' says Keawe, 'I am rich; I will go back and get some money from my wife, who keeps it.'

'That's a bad idea, mate.' said the boatswain. 'Never you trust a petticoat with dollars. They're all as false as water; you keep an eye on her.'

Now this word struck in Keawe's mind; for he was muddled with what he had been drinking.

'I should not wonder but she was false, indeed,' thought he. 'Why else should she be so cast down at my release? But I will show her I am not the man to be fooled. I will catch her in the act.'

Accordingly, when they were back in town, Keawe bade the boatswain wait for him at the corner, by the old calaboose, and went forward up the avenue alone to the door of his house. The night had come again; there was a light within, but never a sound; and Keawe crept about the corner, opened the back door softly, and looked in.

There was Kokua on the floor, the lamp at her side;

before her was a milk-white bottle, with a round belly and a long neck; and as she viewed it, Kokua wrung her hands.

A long time Keawe stood and looked in the doorway. At first he was struck stupid; and then fear fell upon him that the bargain had been made amiss, and the bottle had come back to him as it came at San Francisco; and at that his knees were loosened, and the fumes of the wine departed from his head like mists off a river in the morning. And then he had another thought; and it was a strange one, that made his cheeks to burn.

'I must make sure of this,' thought he.

So he closed the door, and went softly round the corner again, and then came noisily in, as though he were but now returned. And, lo! by the time he opened the front door no bottle was to be seen; and Kokua sat in a chair and started up like one awakened out of sleep.

'I have been drinking all day and making merry,' said Keawe. 'I have been with good companions, and now I only came back for money, and return to drink and carouse with them again'

Both his face and voice were as stern as judgment, but Kokua was too troubled to observe.

'You do well to use your own, my husband,' said she, and her words trembled.

'Oh, I do well in all things,' said Keawe, and he went straight to the chest and took out money. But he looked beside in the corner where they kept the bottle, and there was the bottle there.

At that the chest heaved upon the floor like a sea-billow, and the house spun about him like a wreath of smoke, for he saw she was lost now, and there was no escape. 'It is what I feared,' he thought. 'It is she who has bought it.'

And then he came to himself a little and rose up; but

the sweat streamed on his face as thick as the rain and cold as the well-water.

'Kokua,' said he, 'I said to you today what ill became me. Now I return to house with my jolly companions,' and at that he laughed a little quietly. 'I will take more pleasure in the cup if you forgive me.'

She clasped his knees in a moment, she kissed his knees with flowing tears.

'Oh,' she cried, 'I ask but a kind word!'

'Let us never one think hardly of the other,' said Keawe, and was gone out of the house.

Now, the money that Keawe had taken was only some of that store of centime pieces they had laid in at their arrival. It was very sure he had no mind to be drinking. His wife had given her soul for him, now he must give his for hers; no other thought was in the world with him.

At the corner, by the old calaboose, there was the boatswain waiting.

'My wife has the bottle,' said Keawe, 'and, unless you help me to recover it, there can be no more money and no more liquor tonight.'

'You do not mean to say you are serious about that bottle?' cried the boatswain.

'There is the lamp,' said Keawe. 'Do I look as if I was jesting?'

'That is so,' said the boatswain. 'You look as serious as a ghost.'

'Well, then,' said Keawe, 'here are two centimes; you just go to my wife in the house, and offer her these for the bottle, which (if I am not much mistaken) she will give you instantly. Bring it to me here, and I will buy it back from you for one; for that is the law with this bottle, that it still must be sold for a less sum. But whatever you do, never breathe a word to her that you have come from me.'

'Mate, I wonder arc you making a fool of me?' asked the boatswain.

'It will do you no harm if I am,' returned Keawe.

'That is so, mate,' said the boatswain.

'And if you doubt me,' added Keawe, 'you can try. As soon as you are clear of the house, wish to have your pocket full of money, or a bottle of the best rum, or what you please, and you will see the virtue of the thing.'

'Very well, Kanaka,' says the boatswain. 'I will try; but if you are having your fun out of me, I will take my fun out of you with a belaying-pin.'

So the whale-man went off up the avenue; and Keawe stood and waited. It was near the same spot where Kokua had waited the night before; but Keawe was more resolved, and never faltered in his purpose; only his soul was bitter with despair.

It seemed a long time he had to wait before he heard a voice singing in the darkness of the avenue. He knew the voice to be the boatswain's; but it was strange how drunken it appeared upon a sudden.

Next the man himself came stumbling into the light of the lamp. He had the devil's bottle buttoned in his coat; another bottle was in his hand; and even as he came in view he raised it to his mouth and drank.

'You have it,' said Keawe. 'I see that.'

'Hands off!' cried the boatswain, jumping back. 'Take a step near me, and I'll smash your mouth. You thought you could make a catspaw of me, did you?'

'What do you mean?' cried Keawe.

'Mean?' cried the boatswain. 'This is a pretty good bottle, this is; that's what I mean. How I got it for two centimes I can't make out; but I am sure you shan't have it for one.'

'You mean you won't sell?' gasped Keawe.

'No, sir,' cried the boatswain. 'But I'll give you a

drink of the rum if you like.'

'I tell you,' said Keawe, 'the man who has that bottle goes to hell.'

'I reckon I'm going anyway,' returned the sailor; 'and this bottle's the best thing to go with I've struck yet. No, sir!' he cried again, 'this is my bottle now, and you can go and fish for another.'

'Can this be true?' Keawe cried. 'For your own sake, I beseech you, sell it me!'

'I don't value any of your talk,' replied the boatswain. 'You thought I was a flat, now you see I'm not; and there's an end. If you won't have a swallow of the rum, I'll have one myself. Here's your health, and good-night to you!'

So off he went down the avenue towards town, and there goes the bottle out of the story.

But Keawe ran to Kokua light as the wind; and great was their joy that night; and great, since then, has been the peace of all their days in the Bright House.

The Apple of Trouble

JOAN AIKEN

It was a black day for the Armitage family when Great-Uncle Gavin retired. In fact, as Mark pointed out, Uncle Gavin did not exactly retire; he was pushed. He had been High Commissioner of Mbutam-Mbuta-land, which had suddenly decided it needed a High Commissioner no longer, but would instead become the Republic of Mbutambutala. So Sir Gavin Armitage K.C.M.G., O.B.E., D.S.O. and so forth, was suddenly turned loose on the world, and because he had expected to continue living at the High Commissioner's Residence for years to come, and had no home of his own, he moved in with the parents of Mark and Harriet.

The first disadvantage was that he had to sleep in the ghost's room. Mr Peake was nice about it, he said he quite understood, and they would probably shake down together very well, he had been used to all sorts of odd company in his three hundred years. But after a few weeks of Great-Uncle Gavin's keep-fit exercises, coughing, thumping, harrumphing, snoring, and blazing open windows, Mr Peake became quite thin and pale (for a ghost); he migrated through the wall into the room next door, explaining apologetically that he wasn't getting a wink of sleep. Unfortunately the room next door was a bathroom, and though Mark didn't mind, Mr Armitage complained that it gave him the jumps to see a ghostly face suddenly loom up beside his in the mirror when he was shaving, while Harriet and her mother had to take to the downstairs bathroom. Great-Uncle Gavin never noticed Mr Peake at all. He was not sensitive. Besides he had other things to think about.

One of his main topics of thought was how disgracefully the children had been brought up. He was horrified at the way they were allowed to live all over the house, instead of being pent in some upstairs nursery.

'Little gels should be seen and not heard,' he boomed at Harriet whenever she opened her mouth. To get her out from underfoot during the holidays he insisted on her enrolling in a domestic science course run by a Professor Grimalkin who had recently come to live in the village.

As for Mark, he had hardly a minute's peace.

'God bless my soul, boy'—nearly all Great-Uncle Gavin's remarks began with this request—'God bless my soul, what are you doing now? Reading? God bless my soul, do you want to grow up a muff?'

'A muff, Great-Uncle? What is a muff, exactly?' And Mark pulled out the notebook in which he was keeping a glossary of Great-Uncle Gavin.

'A muff, why, a muff is a—a funk, sir, a duffer, a frowst, a tug, a swot, a miserable little sneaking milksop!'

Mark was so busy writing down all these words that he forgot to be annoyed.

'You ought to be out of doors, sir, ought to be out playin' footer.'

'But you need twenty-two people for that,' Mark pointed out, 'and there's only Harriet and me. Besides it's summer. And Harriet's a bit of a duffer at French cricket.'

'Don't be impident, boy! Gad, when I was your age I'd have been out collectin' birds' eggs.'

'Birds' eggs,' said Mark, scandalised. 'But I'm a subscribing member of the Royal Society for the Protection of Birds.'

'Butterflies, then,' growled his great-uncle.

'I read a book, Great-Uncle, that said all the butterflies were being killed by indiscriminate use of pesticides and what's left ought to be carefully preserved.'

Sir Gavin was turning eggplant colour and seemed likely to explode.

'Boy's a regular sea-lawyer,' he said furiously. 'Grow up into one of those confounded trade-union johnnies. Why don't you go out on your velocipede, then, sir? At your age I was as keen as mustard, by gad; used to ride miles on my penny-farthing, rain or shine.'

'No bike,' said Mark. 'Only the unicorn, and he's got a swelled fetlock; we're fomenting it.'

'Unicorn! Never heard such namby-pamby balderdash in my life! Here,' Great-Uncle Gavin said, 'what's your weekly allowance when your pater's at home?'

With the disturbed family ghost and the prospect of Uncle Gavin's indefinite stay to depress them, Mr and Mrs Armitage had rather meanly decided that they were in need of three weeks in Madeira and had left the day before.

'Half a crown a week,' said Mark. 'I've had three weeks in advance.'

'How much does a bike cost nowadays?'

'Oh, I dare say you could pick one up for thirty-five pounds.'

'What?' Great-Uncle Gavin nearly fell out of his chair, but then, rallying, he pulled seven five-pound notes out of his ample wallet. 'Here, then, boy; this is an advance on yer allowance for the next two hundred and eighty weeks. I'll collect it from your governor when he comes home. Cut along, now, and buy a bicycle, an' go for a topping spin and don't let me see your face again till suppertime.'

'But I don't want a bicycle,' Mark said.

'Be off, boy, make yourself scarce, don't argue!—On second thoughts, 'spose I'd better come with you, to make sure you don't spend the money on some appallin' book about nature.'

So Great-Uncle Gavin stood over Mark while the latter unwillingly and furiously purchased a super-excellent low-slung bicycle with independent suspension, disc brakes, three-inch tyres, five-speed, and an outboard motor. None of which assets did Mark want in the least, as who would when they had a perfectly good unicorn to ride?

'Now be off with you and see how quickly you can get to Brighton and back.'

Day after day thereafter, no sooner had breakfast been eaten than Mark was hounded from the house by his relentless great-uncle and urged to try and better his yesterday's time to Brighton.

'Gosh, he must have led those Mbutam-Mbutas a life,' Mark muttered darkly in the privacy of Harriet's room.

'I suppose he's old and we ought to be patient with him,' Harriet said. She was pounding herbs in a mortar for her domestic science homework.

The trouble was, concluded Mark, gloomily pedalling along one afternoon through a heavy summer downpour, that during his forty years among the simple savages Great-Uncle Gavin had acquired the habit of command; it was almost impossible not to obey his orders.

Almost impossible; not quite. Presently the rain increased to a cloudburst.

'Drat Great-Uncle Gavin! I'm not going all the way to Brighton in this,' Mark decided. 'Anyway, why *should* I go to Brighton?'

And he climbed a stile and dashed up a short grassy path to a small nearby church which had a convenient and dry-looking porch. He left his bike on the other side of the stile, for that is another disadvantage of bikes; you can never take them all the way to where you want to go.

The church proved to be chilly and not very interesting so Mark, who always carried a paperback in his pocket, settled on the porch bench to read until the rain abated. After a while, hearing footsteps, he looked up and saw that a smallish, darkish, foreign-looking man had joined him.

'Nasty afternoon,' Mark said civilly.

'Eh? Yes? Yes, indeed.' The man seemed nervous; he kept glancing over his shoulder down the path.

'Is your bicycle, boy, by wall yonder?' he asked by and by.

'Yes it is.'

'Is a fine one,' the man said. 'Very fine one. Would go lickety-spit fast, I dare say?'

'An average of twenty m.p.h.' Mark said gloomily.

'Will it? Will it so?'

The little man fell silent, glancing out uneasily once more at the rainy dusk, while Mark strained his eyes to see the print of his book. He noticed that his companion seemed to be shuffling about, taking a pack off his back and rummaging among the contents; presently Mark realised that something was being held out to him. He looked up from the page and saw a golden apple—quite a large one, about the size of a Bramley. On one side the gold had a reddish bloom, as if the sun had ripened it. The other side was paler. Somebody had taken two bites out of the red side; Mark wondered what it had done to their teeth. Near the stalk was a dark-brown stain, like a patch of rust.

'Nice, eh?' the little man said, giving the apple to Mark, who nearly dropped it on the flagged floor. It must have weighed at least four pounds.

'Is it real gold all through?' he asked. 'Must be quite valuable?'

'Valuable?' the man said impressively. 'Such apple is beyond price. You of course well-educated, familiar with Old Testament tale of Adam and Eve?'

'W-why yes,' Mark said, stammering a little. 'But you—you don't mean to say that apple . . .?'

'Selfsame one,' the little man said, nodding his head. 'Original bite marks of Adam and Eve before apple carried out of Eden. Then—see stain? Blood of Abel. Cain killed him for apple. Stain will never wash off.'

'Goodness,' Mark said.

'Not all, however—not at all all! Apple of Discord—golden apple same which began Trojan War—have heard of such?'

'Why, yes. But—but you're not telling me . . .'

'Identical apple,' the little man said proudly. 'Apples of Asgard, too? Heard of? Scandinavian golden apples of perpetual youth, guarded by Idhunn?'

'Yes, but you don't . . .'

'Such was one of those. Not to mention Apples of Hesperides, stolen by Hercules.'

'Hold on—surely it couldn't have been both?'

'Could,' the little man said. 'Was. William Tell's apple—familiar story?—same apple. Newton—apple fell on head, letting in dangerous principle of gravity. This. Atalanta—apple thrown by Venus to stop her winning race. Also. Prince Ahmed's apple . . .'

'Stop, stop!' said Mark. 'I don't understand how it could possibly be all those.'

But somehow, as he held the heavy, shining thing in his hand, he did believe the little man's story. There was a peculiar, rather nasty fascination about the apple. It scared him, and yet he wanted it.

'So, see,' the little man said, nodding more than ever, 'worth millions pounds. No lie—millions. And yet I give to you . . .'

'Now, wait a minute . . .'

'Give in exchange for bicycle, Yes? Okay?'

'Well, but—but why? Why don't you want the apple?'

'Want bicycle more.' He glanced down the road again, and now Mark guessed.

'Someone's after you—the police? You stole the apple?'

'Not stole, no, no, no! Did swap, like with bicycle, you agree, yes?'

He was already half-way down the path. Hypnotised, Mark watched him climb the style and mount the bike, wobbling. Suddenly Mark found his voice and called,

'What did you swap for it?'

'Drink of water—in desert, see?'

'Who's chasing you, then?'

By now the little man was chugging down the road and his last word, indistinct, floated back through the rain, something ending in -ese; it might have been Greek for all Mark could make of it.

He put the apple in his pocket, which sagged under the weight, and, since the shower was slackening, walked to the road to flag a lift home in the next lorry.

Great-Uncle Gavin nearly burst a blood vessel when he learned that Mark had exchanged his new bicycle for an apple, albeit a gold one.

'Did what—merciful providence—an apple?—Hesperides? Eden? Asgard? Never heard such a pack of moonshine in all me born—let's see it then. Where is it?'

Mark produced the apple and a curious gleam lit up Uncle Gavin's eye.

'Mind,' he said, 'don't believe a word of the feller's tale, but plain that's val'ble; far too val'ble an article to be in your hands, boy. Better give it here at once. I'll get Christies to value it. And of course we must advertise in *The Times* for the wallah who palmed it off on you—highly illegal transaction, I dare say.'

Mark felt curiously relieved to be rid of the apple, as if a load had been lifted from his mind as well as his pocket.

He ran upstairs whistling. Harriet, as usual, was up in her room mixing things in retorts and crucibles. When Uncle Gavin, as in duty bound, asked each evening what she had been learning that day in her domestic science course, she always replied briefly, 'Spelling.' 'Spellin', gel? Rum notion of housekeepin' the johnny seems to have. Still, dare say it keeps you out of mischief.' In fact, as Harriet had confided to Mark, Professor Grimalkin was a retired alchemist who, having failed to find the Philosopher's Stone, was obliged to take in pupils to make ends meet. He was not a very good teacher; his heart wasn't in it. Mark watched Harriet toss a pinch of green powder into a boiling beaker. Half a peach tree shot up, wavered, sagged, and then collapsed. Impatiently Harriet tipped the frothing liquid out of the window and put some more water on to boil.

Then she returned to the window and peered out into the dark.

'Funny,' she said. 'There seem to be some people waiting outside the front door. Can't think why they didn't ring the bell. Could you let them in, Mark? My hands are all covered with prussic acid. I expect they're friends of Uncle Gavin's.'

Mark went down and opened the door. Outside, dimly illuminated by the light from the porch, he saw three ladies. They seemed to be dressed in old-fashioned clothes, drainpipe skirts down to their ankles, and cloaks and bonnets rather like those of Salvation Army lasses; the bonnets were perched on thick, lank masses of hair. Mark didn't somehow care for their faces which resembled those of dogs—but not tame domestic dogs so much as starved, wild, slightly mad dogs; they stared at Mark hungrily.

'Er—I'm so sorry. Did you ring? Have you been waiting long?' he said.

'A long, long time. Since the world-tree was but a seed in darkness. We are the daughters of Night,' one of them hollowly replied. She moved forward with a leathery rustle.

'Oh.' Mark noticed that she had bat's wings. He stepped back a little. 'Do you want to see Great-Uncle —Sir Gavin Armitage? Won't you come in?'

'Nay. We are the watchers by the threshold. Our place is here.'

'Oh, all right. What name shall I say?'

To this question they replied in a sort of gloomy chant, taking it in turns to speak.

'We are the avengers of blood.'

'Sisters of the nymph with the apple-bough, Nemesis.'

'We punish the sin of child against parent . . .'

'Youth against age . . .'

'Brother against brother . . .'

'We are the Erinnyes, the Kindly Ones . . .' (But their expressions were far from kindly, Mark thought.)

'Tisiphone . . .'

'Alecto . . .'

'And Megaera.'

'And what did you wish to see Sir Gavin about?' Mark knew his great-uncle hated to be disturbed once he was settled in the evening with a glass of port and *The Times*.

'We attend him who holds the apple.'

'There is blood on it—a brother's blood, shed by a brother.'

'It cries for vengeance.'

'Oh, I see!' said Mark, beginning to take in the situation. Now he understood why the little man had been so anxious for a bicycle. 'But, look here, dash it all, Uncle Gavin hasn't shed any blood. That was Cain, and it was a long time ago. I don't see why Uncle should be responsible.'

'He holds the apple.'

'He must bear the guilt.'

'The sins of the fathers are visited on the children.'

'Blood calls for blood.'

Then the three wolfish ladies disconcertingly burst

into a sort of hymn, shaking tambourines and beating on them with brass-studded rods which they pulled out from among their draperies:

'We are the daughters
Of darkness and time
We follow the guilty
We punish the crime
Nothing but bloodshed
Will settle old scores
So blood has to flow and
That blood must be yours!'

When they had finished they fixed their ravenous eyes on Mark again and the one called Alecto said, 'Where is he?'

Mark felt greatly relieved that Uncle Gavin had taken the apple away from him and was therefore apparently responsible for its load of guilt, but as this was a mean thought he tried to stifle it. Turning (not that he liked having the ladies behind his back) he went into the sitting-room where Uncle Gavin was sitting snug by the fire and said,

'There are some callers asking for you, Great-Uncle.'

'God bless my soul, at this time of the evenin'? Who the deuce . . .'

Great-Uncle Gavin crossly stumped out to the porch, saying over his shoulder, 'Why didn't you ask 'em in, boy? Not very polite to leave 'em standing . . .'

Then he saw the ladies and his attitude changed. He said sharply, 'Didn't you see the notice on the gate, my good women? It says No Hawkers or Circulars. I give handsome cheques to charity each year at Christmas and make it a rule never to contribute to door-to-door collections. So be off, if you please!'

'We do not seek money,' Tisiphone hungrily replied.

'Milk-bottle-tops, jumble, old gold, it's all the same. Pack of meddlesome old maids—I've no time for you!' snapped Sir Gavin. 'Good night!' And he shut the door smartly in their faces.

'Have to be firm with that sort of customer,' he told Mark. 'Become a thorough nuisance otherwise—tiresome old harpies. Got wind of that golden apple, I dare say—shows what happens when you mix with such people. Shockin' mistake. Take the apple to Christies tomorrow. Now, please see I'm not disturbed again.' And he returned to the sitting-room.

Mark looked uneasily at the front door but it remained shut; evidently the three Kindly Ones were content to wait outside. But there they stayed; when

Mark returned to Harriet's room he looked out of the window and saw them, sombre and immovable, in the shadows outside the porch, evidently prepared to sit out the night.

'Not very nice if they're going to picket our front door from now on,' he remarked gloomily to Harriet. 'Goodness knows what the postman will think. And *I* don't fancy 'em above half. Wonder how we can get rid of them.'

'I've an idea,' Harriet said. 'Professor Grimalkin was talking about them the other day. They are the Furies. But it's awfully hard to shake them off once they're after you.'

'That's gay.'

'There are various things you can do: biting off your finger . . .'

'Some hope of Uncle Gavin doing that!'

'Or shaving your head.'

'Wouldn't be much use, since he's bald as a bean already.'

'You can bathe seven times in running water or the blood of pigs . . .'

'He always does take a lot of cold baths and we had pork for supper, so plainly that's no go.'

'Well, you can go into exile for a year,' Harriet said.

'I only wish he would.'

'Or build them a grotto, nice and dark, preferably under an ilex tree, and make suitable offerings.'

'Such as what?'

'Anything black, or they rather go for iris flowers. Milk and honey too. And they can be shot with a bow of horn, but that doesn't seem to be very successful as a rule.'

'Oh well, let's try the milk-and-honey and something black for now,' Mark said. 'And I'll make a bow of horn tomorrow—I've got Candleberry's last year's horn in my room somewhere.' Candleberry was the unicorn.

Harriet therefore collected a black velvet pincushion and a bowl of milk and honey. These she put out on the front step, politely wishing the Daughters of Night good evening, to which their only response was a baleful silence.

Next morning the milk and honey was still there. So were the Furies. Evidently they did not intend to be placated so easily. By daylight they were even less prepossessing, having black claws, bloodshot eyes, and snakes for hair. However, slipping down early to remove the saucer in case the postman tripped over it, Harriet did notice that all the pins had been removed from the pincushion. And eaten? This was encouraging. So was the fact that when the postman arrived with a card from parents in Madeira—*Having wonderful time hope you are behaving yourselves*—he walked clean through the Furies without noticing them at all. Evidently his conscience at least was clear.

'Perhaps they're only visible to relatives of their victim,' Harriet suggested to Mark, who was working on the unicorn horn with emery paper.

'I hope they've taken the pins to stick in Uncle Gavin,' he growled. In default of bicycle exercise Great-Uncle Gavin had made Mark do five hundred press-ups before breakfast and had personally supervised the operation. Mark felt it would be far, far better to shoot Uncle Gavin than the Furies who, after all, were only doing their duty.

The most annoying thing of all was that, after his initial interview with them, Uncle Gavin seemed not to notice the avenging spirits at all ('He only sees what he chooses to,' Harriet guessed) and walked past them them quite as unconcernedly as the postman had. He packed up the golden apple in a cigar-box, rang for a taxi, and departed to London. The Furies followed him in a black, muttering group, and were seen no more for several hours; Mark and Harriet heaved sighs of relief. Prematurely, though; at teatime the Furies reappeared, even blacker, muttering still more, and took up their post once more by the front door.

'Lost the old boy somewhere in London,' Mark diagnosed. 'Or perhaps they were chucked out of Christies.'

The unwanted guests were certainly in a bad mood. This time they were accompanied by a smallish thickset winged serpent or dragon who seemed to be called Ladon. Harriet heard them saying, 'Down, Ladon! Behave yourself, and soon you shall sup on blood.' Ladon too seemed to have a snappish disposition, and nearly took off Harriet's hand when she stooped to pat him on returning home from her domestic science lesson.

'What a beautiful green his wings are. Is he yours?' she said to the Furies politely.

'He is the guardian of the apple; he but waits for his own,' Tisiphone replied dourly.

Ladon did not share the Furies' scruples about coming indoors; evidently he was used to a warmer clime and found the doorstep too draughty. He followed Harriet into the kitchen and flopped his bulky length in front of the stove, hissing cantankerously at anyone who came near, and thoroughly upsetting Walrus, the cat.

Walrus was not the only one.

'Miss Harriet! Get that nasty beast out of here at once!' exclaimed Mrs Epis the cook when she came back from shopping. 'And what those black ladies are doing out on the front door step I'm sure I don't know; I've two or three times give them a hint to be off but they won't take it.'

Evidently Mrs Epis counted as one of the family or else she, too, had a guilty conscience. Mark and Harriet soon found that visitors to the house who had episodes in their past of which they had cause to be ashamed were apt to notice the Erinnyes in a patchy, nervous way and hurry away with uneasy glances behind them, or else break into sudden and embarrassing confessions.

And Ladon was a thorough nuisance. So long as Harriet kept on the fan heater in her room he would lie in front of it, rolling luxuriously on his back and only snapping if anyone approached him. But at bedtime when she turned the fan off—for she hated a warm room at night—he became fretful and roamed snarling and clanking about the house. Even Uncle Gavin tripped over him then and blamed the children furiously for leaving what he thought was a rolled-up tent lying in the passage.

'Things can't go on like this,' Mark said despondently.

'We've certainly got to get rid of them all somehow before Mother and Father come home next week,' Harriet agreed. 'And Uncle Gavin's plainly going to be no help at all.'

Uncle Gavin was even more tetchy than usual. Christies had sent him a letter saying that in view of the apple's unique historical interest it was virtually impossible to put a price on it, but in their opinion it was certainly worth well over a million pounds. They would return the apple by the next registered post pending further instructions. And the advertisement which appeared in *The Times* every day, 'Will person who persuaded young boy to exchange valuable new bicycle for metal apple on August 20 please contact Box—' was producing no replies.

'Nor likely to,' Mark said. 'That chap knows when he's well out of trouble.'

During that day Mark finished his horn bow and tried shooting at the Furies with it. The operation was a total failure. The arrows, which he had decided to make from a fallow-deer's antler (brow, bay, and tray) were curved, and flew on a bias, like bowls, missing the visitors nine times out of ten. If they did hit they merely passed clean through and, as Mark told Harriet later, he felt a fool having to pick them up under the malign snaky-and-bonneted gaze of Alecto, Megaera, and Tisiphone.

Harriet, however, came home in good spirits. She pulled out and showed Mark a paper covered with Professor Grimalkin's atrocious handwriting.

'What is it?' he asked.

'Recipe for a friendship philtre. You've heard of a love philtre? This is like that, only milder. I'm going to try it in their milk. Now don't interrupt, while I make it up.'

She put her crucible on to bubble. Mark curled up at the end of her bed and read his bird book, only coming out when Harriet tripped over Ladon and dratted him, or asked Mark's opinion about the professor's handwriting.

'Is this verdigris or verjuice, do you think? And is that Add sugar, or Allow to simmer?'

'It'll be a miracle if the stuff turns out all right,' Mark said pessimistically. 'Anyway, do we want the Furies friendly?'

'Of course we do, it'll be a tremendous help. Where was I now? Add bad egg, and brown under grill.'

Finally the posion was finished and put in a cough-mixture bottle. ('It smells awful,' Mark said, sniffing. 'Never mind, how do we know what *they* like?') A spoonful of the noxious stuff was divided between three bowls of milk, which were placed on the front step, at the feet of the unresponsive Erinnyes.

However, after a moment or two they began to snuff the air like bloodhounds on the track of a malefactor, and as Harriet tactfully retired she had the pleasure of seeing all three of them lapping hungrily at the mixture. So far, at least, the spell had worked. Harriet went hopefully to bed.

Next morning she was woken by a handful of earth flung at her window.

'Miss Harriet!' It was Mrs Epis on the lawn. 'Miss Harriet you'll have to make the breakfast yourself. I'm taking a week's holiday. And things had better be different when I come back or I'll give in my notice; you can tell your Ma it was me broke the Crown Derby teapot and I'm sorry about it, but there's some things a body can't bear. Now I'm off home.'

Sleepy and mystified, Harriet went to the kitchen to put on the kettle for Great-Uncle Gavin's tea. There, to her dismay, she found the Furies, who greeted her with toothy smiles. They were at ease in basket chairs round the stove, with their long skirts turned back so as to toast their skinny legs and feet, which rested on Ladon. Roused by the indoor warmth, the snakes on their heads were in a state of disagreeable squirm and writhe which Harriet too found hard to bear, particularly before breakfast; she quite sympathised with the cook's departure.

'Oh, good morning,' she said, however, stoutly controlling her qualms. 'Would you like some more milk?' She mixed another brew with potion (which was graciously accepted) and took up a tray of breakfast to Great-Uncle Gavin, explaining that Mrs Epis had been called away. By the time she returned, Mark was in the kitchen, glumly taking stock of the situation.

'Feel like a boiled egg?' Harriet said.

'I'll do it, thanks, I've had enough of your domestic science.'

They ate their boiled eggs in the garden. But they had taken only a bite or two when they were startled by hysterical screams from the window-cleaner who, having arrived early and started work on the kitchen window, had looked through the glass and was now on his knees in the flowerbed, confessing to anyone who would listen that he had pinched a diamond brooch from an upstairs bedroom in West Croydon. Before he was pacified they had also to deal with the man who came to mend the fridge, who seemed frightfully upset about something he had done to a person called Elsie, as well as a French onion-seller who dropped eight strings of onions in the back doorway and fled, crying, 'Mon Dieu, mon Dieu, mon crime est découvert! Je suis perdu!'

'This won't do,' said Mark, as he returned from escorting the sobbing electrician to the gate. Exhaustedly mopping his brow he didn't look where he was going, barked his shins painfully on Ladon, who was stalking the cat, and let out an oath. It went unheard; the Furies, much cheered by their breakfast and a night spent in the snug kitchen, were singing their bloodthirsty hymn fortissimo, with much clashing of tambourines. Ladon and the cat seemed all set for a duel to the death; and Great-Uncle Gavin was bawling down the stairs for less row while a man was breakfastin', dammit!

'It's all right,' Harriet soothed Mark. 'I knew the potion would work wonders. Now, your Kindlinesses,' she said to the Erinnyes, 'we've got a beautiful grotto ready for you, just the sort of place you like, except I'm sorry there isn't an ilex tree, if you wouldn't mind stepping this way,' and she led them to the coal-cellar, which, being peaceful and dark, met with their entire approval.

'I dare say they'll be glad of a nap,' she remarked, shutting the door thankfully on them. 'After all, they've been unusually busy lately.'

'That's all very well,' said Mark. 'They'd better not stay there long. I'm the one that fetches the coal.

And there's still beastly Ladon to dispose of.'

Ladon, unlike his mistresses, was not tempted by milk containing a friendship potion. His nature remained as intractable as ever. He now had the cat Walrus treed on the banister post at the top of the stairs, and was coiled in a baleful bronze-and-green heap just below, hissing like a pressure-cooker.

'Perhaps bone arrows will work on him,' said Mark, and dashed to his bedroom.

As he reappeared a lot of things happened at once. The postman rang the front-door bell and handed Harriet a letter for Uncle Gavin and a registered parcel labelled GOLD WITH CARE. Ladon made a dart at the cat, who countered with a faster-than-light left hook, all claws extended. It caught the dragon in his gills and he let out a screech like the whistle of a steam locomotive which fetched the Furies from their grotto at the double, brass-studded batons out and snakes ready to strike.

At the same moment Mark let fly with his bow and arrow and Uncle Gavin burst from his bedroom exclaiming, 'I will not have this bedlam while I'm digestin' my breakfast!' He received the arrow intended for Ladon full in his slippered heel and gave a yell which quite drowned the noise made by the cat and dragon.

'Who did that? Who fired that damned thing?' Enraged, hopping, Uncle Gavin pulled out the bone dart. 'What's that cat doin' up there? Why's this confounded reptile in the house? Who are those people down there? *What the devil's going on around here?*'

Harriet gave a shout of joy.

'Look, quick!' she called to the Furies. 'Look at his heel! It's bleeding!' (It was indeed.) 'You said blood had to flow and now it has, so you've done your job and can leave with clear consciences! Quick, Mark, open the parcel and give that wretched dragon his apple and they can all leave. Poor Uncle Gavin, is your foot very painful? Mark didn't mean to hit you. I'll bandage it up in two shakes.'

Mark tore the parcel undone and tossed the golden apple to Ladon, who caught it with a snap of his jaws and was gone in a flash through the landing window. (It was shut, but no matter.) At the same moment the Furies, their lust for vengeance appeased by the sight of Uncle Gavin's gore, departed with more dignity by the front door.

Alecto even turned and gave Harriet a ghastly smile.

'Thank you for having us, child,' she said. 'We enjoyed our visit.'

'Don't mention it,' Harriet mechanically replied, and only just stopped herself from adding, 'Come again.'

Then she sat her great-uncle in the kitchen arm-chair and bathed his heel. The wound, luckily, proved to be no more than a scratch. While she bandaged it he read his letter, and suddenly gave a curious grunt of pleasure and astonishment.

'God bless my soul! They want me back! Would you believe it!'

'Who want you back, Great-Uncle?' Harriet asked, tying the ends of the bandage in a knot.

'The Mbutam-Mbutas, bless 'em! They want me to go and help 'em as Military and Economic Adviser. I've always said there's good in the black feller and I say so yet! Well, well, well! Don't know when I've been so pleased.' He gave his nose a tremendous blow and wiped his eyes.

'Oh, Uncle Gavin, how perfectly splendid!' Harriet gave him a hug. 'When do they want you to go?'

'Three weeks' time. Bless my soul I'll have a bustle getting me kit ready.'

'Oh, we'll all help like mad. I'll run down the road now and fetch Mrs Epis; I'm sure she'll be glad to come back for such an emergency.'

Mrs Epis had no objection at all, once she was assured the intruders were gone from the house.

Harriet had one startled moment when they got back.

'Uncle Gavin!' she called, and ran upstairs. The old gentleman had out his tin tropical trunk and was inspecting a pith helmet. 'Yes, m'dear, what is it?' he said absently.

'The little brown bottle on the kitchen table. Was it—did you . . .?'

'Oh, that? My cough mixture? Yes, I finished it and threw the bottle away. Why, though, bless my soul—*there's* my cough mixture! What the deuce have I been an' taken, then, gel? Anything harmful?'

'Oh no, perfectly harmless,' Harriet hastily reassured him. 'Now, you give me anything you want mended and I'll be getting on with it.'

''Pon me soul,' Uncle Gavin said, pulling out a bundle of spotless white ducks and a dress jacket with tremendous epaulettes and fringes, ''pon my soul, I believe I'll miss you young ones when I'm back in the tropics. Come and visit me sometimes, m'dear? Young Mark too. Where is the young rogue? Ho, ho, can't help laughing when I think how he hit me in the heel. Who'd have thought he had it in him?'

'He's gone apple-picking at the farm down the road,' Harriet explained. 'He wants to earn enough to pay back that thirty-five pounds.'

'Good lad, good lad!' Uncle Gavin exclaimed approvingly. 'Not that he need have bothered, mark you.'

And in fact, when Mark tried to press the money on Uncle Gavin at his departure, he would have none of it.

'No, no, bless your little hearts, split it between you.'

He chucked Harriet under the chin and earnestly shook Mark's hand. 'I'd never have thought' I'd cotton to young 'uns as I have to you two—'mazing thing. So you keep the money and buy something pretty to remind you of my visit.'

But Mark and Harriet thought they would remember his visit quite easily without that—especially as the Furies had taken quite a fancy to the coal-cellar and frequently came back to occupy it on chilly winter nights.

The Sword in the Stone

T. H. WHITE

Probably only the magician, Merlyn, knew that his pupil, the Wart (to rhyme with 'Art') would one day be the great King Arthur.

For six years Merlyn was the boy's tutor and the Wart learned all manner of useful things; such as what it is like to be a fish or a hawk or a badger.

Then the king, Pendragon, died without heirs. And King Pellinore arrived at the court with an extraordinary story of a sword stuck in an anvil stuck to a stone outside a church in London. Written on the sword in gold letters were the words

Whoso Pulleth Out This Sword of
This Stone and Anvil, is Rightwise
King Born of All England.

The last person anybody expected to pull out the sword was the Wart but then he had had Merlyn as his tutor for the past six years.

The Black Cauldron

LLOYD ALEXANDER

Lloyd Alexander is one of America's most distinguished children's authors. He holds both the Newbery Medal and the National Book Award. *The Black Cauldron* is the second book in his Chronicles of Prydain, following *The Book of Three* which is also an Armada Lion.

Once again Taran, the Assistant Pig-Keeper, and his ill-assorted band of followers are led into a world full of humour, enchantment and peril.

The Book of Three

LLOYD ALEXANDER

Lloyd Alexander is one of America's most distinguished children's authors. He holds both the Newbery Medal and the National Book Award. *The Book of Three*, a marvellous blend of mythology and Welsh legend, is the first title in his Chronicles of Prydain. It describes with rich humour and wisdom the adventures and misadventures of Taran, the Assistant Pig-Keeper, who longs to become a hero. His motley band of followers—hideous, hairy Gurgi, fiddler Flam, Doli the invisible dwarf, and the beautiful Princess Eilonwy—are as enchanting as his enemies are terrible.

The second book in the Chronicle, *The Black Cauldron*, is also an Armada Lion.